PF
Or

I just finished reading your powe... u
have in sharing your journey. So many moments of joy & anguish, of trauma
& love. Your honesty and candidness are astounding. And now you're living
the next chapter. May it be filled with deep joy & peace.

Bp. Robert Morneau
—Pastor of Resurrection Parish
—Auxiliary Bishop of Green Bay

Bea Seidl's *Orphan Doors* is a beautifully written memoir that tells a
heartbreaking story of loss, suffering, and forgiveness. After starting to read
it, I couldn't put it down.

David J. Danelski
—Boone Centennial Professor, Emeritus, Stanford University

A compelling story of a woman who overcame adversity. The feelings of
rejection of family, a lost childhood, self confidence, and being raised in an
orphanage, is an emotional story of human survival. Her determination to
overcome, forgive, and live a fruitful, spiritual life is a must read.

Elaine Schultz
—Special Education Teacher

Anyone who ever thought they wanted to be an orphan only needs to read Bea
Seidl's account of her childhood to set their thinking straight. This inspiring
account of her childhood and her years of recovery make a wonderful and
inspiring read.

Tony Staley
—Retired editor of The Compass, newspaper of the Catholic
—Diocese of Green Bay, WI.

The huge orphanage doors frightened six-year-old Bea. In detailing her life story, Bea Seidl has masterfully woven her experiences of abandonment, fear, strength, and forgiveness into an account both startling and redeeming. A rewarding read.

Jackie Staley
—Retired teacher and avid reader

I couldn't put it down. I could hear your voice and read your eyes in every line. Your book is beautiful, comforting, wise and funny. Which is exactly the way I think of you.

Shelia
—Diocesan Co-worker

ORPHAN DOORS

BEA SEIDL

ISBN: 1480037168
ISBN 13: 9781480037168

For my children
And for my sister with love

CONTENTS

Orphan Doors

Tall, gray, scary
Invitations, letdowns
Iron bars, despair
Gold, guilt
You get not to choose

They shape, they form
They lead to other doors
We are what they are
Complacent, uncaring
Faultless, dying

The door closes; there is no escape
No loving touches
Waiting for love to pass through
No cheers
Or guidance

Confidence wavering
Life lying dormant
Where can I find you?
How do I find you?

Hug me when I'm scared
Tonight, tuck me in, stay with me
Read me a story
Give me your shoulder
Tell me it's okay to cry
Show me the way

Share with me beautiful music
Laughter
Soft, furry kittens
God's stars and lightening bugs

Do you love me?
Am I beautiful?

Open the door.
b

The following is a true story, written to the best of my recollection. Any errors in subject matter are mine and not told intentionally or deliberately.

Some of the dialogue may not be exact, but is remembered emotionally and is true to the moment.

All names have been changed with the following exceptions:
My first husband, Ken, our children, his sisters, nieces, and nephews.
My second husband, Jerry, his mom and dad, and his children.
Neighbors in 1966
Co-workers from 1979 to 2008

This is but one *Orphan Doors* story. There are hundreds, thousands of others all over the world.

Bea Seidl

ORPHAN
DOORS

PROLOGUE

January 1982
Green Bay, Wisconsin

I took my time that early January morning turning my car east off Riverside Drive and up the hill to the new location of the Green Bay Diocese's office compound. I wasn't sure I wanted to be there. I was driving toward the site of the old St. Joseph's Orphanage where I had lived eight years of my childhood. Many of my memories of that place and those years were as cold as the day.

More than thirty years had passed since I vowed never to return. I had built a wall of bitterness and resentment, had buried everything I didn't want to remember. I was there now because I worked for Catholic Social Services, formerly the Green Bay Diocese Apostolate. (The Apostolate was the organization that coordinated child welfare services for the Diocese during the 1930s and '40s and beyond.)

As I drove toward Bona Hall, new home of the Social Services office, I tried to recall my first impression in 1942. I remembered a huge building, remembered thinking it must be a castle and princes and princesses must live there. I could still picture the large, rounded windows and the tower with the cross high above. I remembered big trees hiding parts of the building.

I looked to my left. I hadn't noticed the orchard then. Now I nodded at the gnarled, barren trees and chuckled at a memory of kids climbing the trees. *Those could be the same trees we picked apples from and climbed when Sister wasn't watching.*

The driveway curved north past Bona Hall, past the chapel that served the compound, to a large parking lot. I faced west toward the Bungalow (former residence of the orphanage director) and the frozen Fox River as I emerged from my car, a newspaper under my arm. I closed my eyes, envisioning the swings and slide that used to be right about where I was standing. I glanced back at the river. *I remember skating on that river.*

It was still early; I had time to tour the grounds. I made a quick scan of the circle of buildings, brought my coat collar up around my face, and started my round.

The Bungalow hadn't changed, at least not on the outside. I headed north to Melania Hall and wondered about the chance of there still being a laundry there. The crescent cement wall that had stretched from Melania to Bosco Hall was gone. I remembered walking atop it, pretending I was a tightrope walker. The parking lot extended past where the wall had been, but the remaining thicket still obscured what lay beyond, at one time a thriving dairy farm.

I moved toward Bosco Hall (formerly Nazareth Hall, the nursery, or Baby House as it was referred to then) where my younger brother and sister resided during the time when I didn't know where they were. I surmised that much of Bosco would have changed—maybe the gym would be the same.

I distinctly remembered the closet on the third floor. A tall nun dragging me there, locking me in. I could still hear the key's click and feel the black air fold around me. I quickly replaced that image with a happier one of the gym: shiny wooden floors, basketball hoops, boys running, girls cheering.

Just past Bosco I turned east and started up the sidewalk toward Webster Avenue (the outer boundary of the diocesan compound), passing a ranch home (built in 1976) where Bishop Aloysius J. Wycislo lived. At the top was the square, four-story red brick building (the Chancery, which was razed in September 2010) where Bishop Stanislaus V. Bona had resided.

Traffic was just starting to move on Webster. Looking down the sidewalk, I recollected the bumps and bruises that my knees—and other body parts—earned while roller skating up and down a much older sidewalk. As I walked back to the parking lot, I looked south to where snow had been piled high and remembered sleds and toboggans with laughing children.

My survey completed, I headed toward Bona Hall to find where my office would be. Nowhere did I see evidence of St. Joseph's Orphanage, the *fortress* that had once stood here overlooking the Fox River.

The newspaper I was carrying, a *Green Bay Press Gazette*, dated January 6, 1981, included an editorial titled "Landmark Going." It stated:

While all the debate over downtown redevelopment has been going on, another of the area's historic landmarks has been quietly slated for demolition—St. Joseph's Home for Children in Allouez.

The enormous Italianate building has been part of the landscape for a century, home and school for as many as 300 children and built by European immigrants as solidly as the fortress it resembles.

Inside are winding staircases, dovetailed floors and wainscoting of solid hardwood. Tall, transomed doors and pressed-tin ceilings, and enormous oval windows overlooking the Fox River speak of an era before soaring fuel costs.

And now it's coming down, its cupola toppled and the slate roof stripped away.

Next time you're driving down Riverside or Webster, you may want to look up and say goodbye. There won't be anything like it here again.

I was less kind in my assessment of the orphanage. I didn't remember its grand architecture. I only remembered how alone and terrified I was that first day nearly forty years ago.

Such imprints are impossible to erase. Perhaps diminish, but never erase.

PART ONE

All the love we come to know in life springs from the love we knew as children.

—Thoughtful Books Sta-Kris, Inc. 1988

CHAPTER ONE

September 3, 1942
Northeastern Wisconsin
The Journey Begins

I remember feeling pretty in my first new dress as I sat on the front porch of my home. I smoothed wrinkles from the skirt of the garment's robin egg blue fabric. I stretched out my legs and raised my feet, first the right, then the left, so as to better admire my new black–and-white tennis shoes.

I wish Joan could see me. I look just like a princess in one of her storybooks. Where is Joan anyway?

Joan was the first person I saw each morning, but she hadn't been around for two days. She often helped me get dressed. I told her I was old enough to dress myself, but I loved how she babied me. That day my mother Glenda dressed me, but she was in a hurry. She had four other children, including a six-week-old infant, to tend to. The new clothes were for a special occasion she said, without telling me what that special occasion was.

In the early afternoon, my mother ran a comb through my hair and sent me outside. She told me to watch for a black car. Ellen was coming to our house again. (Ellen Johnson, a child welfare worker from the Green Bay Apostolate, was scheduled to arrive in the early afternoon.) I was to go with Ellen but didn't have to talk to her, or anyone else for that matter.

The day was getting warmer, unseasonably hot for Northeastern Wisconsin in early September. I was a rambunctious child, had a difficult time sitting still, would rather be running around the park across the street than sitting on our dumpy porch. I kept calling to my mother through the screen door asking her when Ellen would be here, but she just shushed me and told me to wait outside. By the time Ellen's car pulled up to the front of the house, I was hot and sweaty. Ellen got out of the car, walked up to the front porch, and asked if I was ready to go. I looked for some assurance from my mother as she watched from behind the screen door. When she gave none, I followed Ellen to the car. Ellen opened the passenger side door, pulled the seat forward, and told me to sit in the back.

The back seat was stuffy and hotter than the outdoors. I looked at the windows and wondered how to open them. A cool breeze would feel good. I poked at the seat cushions. They felt hot too, and coarse, and made the skin on the back of my legs itch.

Ellen started the car and soon we left behind the streets of my hometown and made our way northward into the countryside. I tried to get my bearings by leaning back and gazing out the window. All I saw was a scrap of blue sky. I leaned forward to count passing cars, ended up counting eight bobby pins that held Ellen's bun in place. If I looked down, I could see Ellen's briefcase on the front seat. *I wonder what's in it. It looks the same as the one she had when she came to our house before.*

I turned my attention back to the passenger side window. The motor hum grew louder when Ellen opened her window, and I could barely hear her talking to me over the noise.

"Is blue your favorite color?" she asked . . . "Are you excited about school starting?"

Tuning Ellen out, I focused on the passing scenery—the billboards, the towns, the farmhouses, the barns and their silos, and the herds of cows. Everything was a kaleidoscope of blue, gold, and green. I tingled at the sight of horses sprinting along stretches of rail fences. The only horses I'd ever seen were in storybooks. These were real, sleek and shiny, their bushy tails flying straight out when they raced away across the open field. I scrunched my face against the window and imagined being nuzzled by velvety muzzles and running my fingers through silky manes. I rubbernecked till they were out of sight, vowing that one day I'd have my very own horse.

Forty minutes into the journey, the Fox River made its appearance off to the left. Soon the winding river brought us to our destination: CITY OF GREEN BAY, POPULATION 46,205, the sign read. So engrossed was I in the sights, I didn't notice that the car had made a right turn into a long drive.

"We're here." Ellen turned to me and nodded.

I bolted upright, my eyes riveted on the massive structure descending on us as we drove in. Towers and turrets rose above giant trees, rustling leaves played peek-a-boo with large, rounded windows. High atop one of the towers a shiny cross glowed in the afternoon sun.

I leaned against the front seat and thought: *It's a castle! Just like the princess castles in Joan's storybooks.*

The fantasy dissipated as the vehicle neared the huge building, a high-pillared canopy darkening the entryway where the car had stopped. Ellen opened the car door and stepped out.

"Come with me," she said, reaching into the back.

Main entrance, 1970s
Courtesy of the Diocese of Green Bay Archives

Clinging to Ellen's hand, I kept pace with her up the steps of the arched porch where two heavy, wooden doors guarded the entrance to the building.

I tilted my head back to see the top of the tall portal. Ellen pressed the brass button to the right of the doors. Instantly we heard a loud ringing coming from inside. Shortly, one of the doors opened and there stood a nun in the black-and-white habit of the School Sisters of Notre Dame. I balked when Ellen tried to usher me through the doorway. Once inside, I dropped Ellen's hand and backed away from the heavy-set, bespectacled figure.

"This is Sister Agatha," Ellen stated.

I held my ground, close to the open doorway, while Ellen and the nun exchanged some private words. Ellen opened her briefcase and handed Sister Agatha a folder. Walking over to me, she gently touched my shoulder, smiled, said good-bye, and left.

The door, that a moment ago had given way to blue skies and bright sunshine, closed, leaving me alone with Sister Agatha. Her voluminous black wool serge partially hid shadowy hallways and wide, looming staircases.

First floor, center hall, July, 1978
Courtesy of the Diocese of Green Bay Archives

I stood paralyzed. *Where is Ellen going? Where am I? Where is Joan?* I wanted to run, but my feet wouldn't move; I wanted to scream, but my mouth wouldn't open. I flung my arms across the giant wooden entrance that had swallowed me up. Images of my sister, of Ellen, my mother, swept through my mind, slowly faded, and finally succumbed to nothingness. All that was left was the realization that I was alone, abandoned to the monstrous edifice behind the foreboding doors.

"Follow me," Sister Agatha said as she headed into the dark passageway.

CHAPTER TWO

September 3, 1942
The Orphanage
Lonely Night

Sister Agatha looked back when she didn't hear me following. She repeated her command, this time more sternly. I looked up at the nun and shook my head, "No!"

"You come here right now." Sister Agatha pointed to a spot immediately in front of her.

"No," I exclaimed and dodged the nun's outstretched hand as she advanced toward me. I tried to run into a corridor behind Sister Agatha but stopped when I saw a second nun emerging from a hallway's far end.

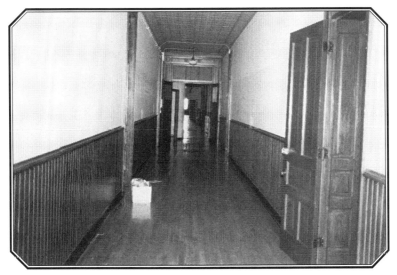

First floor, north hall, July, 1978
Courtesy of the Diocese of Green Bay Archives

Sister Agatha's milky-white hand gripped my arm.

"You go with Sister Edythe now and do as she tells you." Sister Agatha's voice indicated she would put up with no more of my nonsense.

A tall, slender figure approached. Steely blue eyes peered from behind wire-rimmed glasses. The starched wimple made the narrow face and chin appear puffy. She kept her distance, staying arms-length away from her superior. Despite the warm day, I shivered. I didn't like the look in Sister Edythe's eyes.

Saying nothing, Sister Edythe spun around, heading in the direction from where she had come. The corridor was dark. In the shadows I could see other doors on either side of the hallway where the nun was walking, all of them closed. *If only Joan was here, I'd feel safe.*

"Where are we going?" I called after the nun. Sister Edythe still said nothing and kept walking. I ran to catch up with her, not wanting to get lost in the dimly lit maze.

At the far end of the hall, we came to some stairs. We walked up one flight, then another. At the third floor, Sister Edythe nudged me through an open doorway.

The room was painted white, and after the dark hallways and stairs, I had to close my eyes against the bright light. I opened them slowly and looked around at the tiled floors, the showers, and toilets. Orange cakes of soap were the only things not white in the otherwise sterile room. The smooth, oval wedges puddled in the shallow indents of a row of pedestal sinks. A wooden chair was parked under a frosted window. Various items, including some folded towels, took up space on a shelf above a radiator.

Sister Edythe closed the door, pulled the chair to the room's center, and snapped her fingers at me, indicating I was to sit down. I thought otherwise and almost made it to the door before the nun caught me by the arm and forced me into the chair. Producing a pair of scissors, she cut my hair with no thought to any style. It fell to the floor in ragged bunches.

Sister Edythe undressed me and tossed my new dress and shoes away as if they were rags. Before I could object, the nun motioned me into a shower where she proceeded to scrub me from head to toes.

Out of the shower, I sneezed as she raked a powdery substance through what remained of my hair. "What's that stuff for," I asked, but she didn't answer. I stared defiantly at her and ran my fingers through my former shoulder-length hair which now resembled a Prince Valiant botch-job. Sister Edythe handed me a pair of underpants and stockings, which I slipped into immediately. She pointed to a pair of shoes by the radiator and spoke for the first time. "Put those on.

"Your clothes will have to be burned," she continued, as she took a dress from the radiator shelf and held it out to me.

"No," I objected sharply. "I want my own dress. Why can't I have my own dress? It was brand new. I want Joan to see it."

When Sister Edythe grabbed at me again, I ducked into a nearby corner, yanked the dress over my head, and crammed my feet into the shoes.

Satisfied that I was fully dressed, Sister Edythe led the way out of the bathroom to a stairway. "This way," she said.

I shivered, not because I was cold, but because I was scared . . . scared of what was ahead, of the unknown.

We descended to the building's basement level, our silence broken by the sound of talking and laughter, reaching its crescendo at an entrance to a huge room. I froze at the rows of tables and chairs filled with boys and girls of various ages; there had to be over two hundred kids. Arms and hands moved in waves as spoons clanged against white bowls and mugs came down on the wooden tables. Some of the chatter stopped, and it felt like all eyes were following Sister Edythe and me to an empty chair at the dining room's far end.

Basement dining room, July, 1978
Courtesy of the Diocese of Green Bay Archives

When Sister made sure I had seated myself, she disappeared. She returned a few minutes later with a bowl of soup and a cup of milk and placed the food in front of me.

I pushed the bowl away and folded my hands in my lap. "I'm not gonna stay here. I wanna go home," I said to no one in particular. I thought about home, my new baby brother, and how I missed Joan.

My daydream was broken by the scraping of chairs as children got up to leave the dining room. A few remained to clear the tables, roll carts of dirty dishes away, and reset the tables.

"You skipped one over here," one girl yelled to another who was banging cups and bowls upside down on the tables.

"Shhh." A nun—all in white, a hint of a smile on her lined face—hustled in and walked over to the first girl. "Mary, straighten those spoons and make sure they're even with the edge of the table. And Jody, stop setting those dishes down so hard, you'll break them."

I slunk further into my chair when I saw Sister Edythe approach. The nun scowled at the untouched soup. "I've no time for this foolishness," she said to me. "Go hungry if you want. Come along now."

We navigated down more endless corridors past closets and open rooms. In one of the rooms, some boys were playing Ping-Pong. We came to a set of double doors beyond which was a room at least as large as the dining room.

A row of ground-level windows did little to light what appeared to be a playroom. The perimeter was filled with tables and chairs of various sizes, most with girls sitting at them, some reading. Eight or nine girls were jammed together on two couches watching two more girls fiddle with the knobs of a wooden console radio. At a square table, a young nun and three girls flicked small, donut-shaped disks around a wooden board while others watched. Groups of girls played jacks on the linoleum floor. Sister Edythe walked across the room, stopped to talk to the other nun, and disappeared out a far door.

I slumped into a chair near the playroom doors and turned on my best pout. When no one paid any attention, I puckered up, hoping tears would fall. "Joan will come," I whispered. "She'll take me home."

A girl with large, gray-blue eyes walked over to me and stared at me for a few seconds. "Hi, do you wanna play a game?" she asked.

I didn't answer. The girl tried again, "I have some Miss America cutouts."

When I looked the other way, the girl persisted. "My name is Emma. It's really Emily, but everybody calls me Emma. My birthday is in November. I'll be seven. What's your name? How old are you?"

While I continued my pout, Emma danced in front of me, her eyes sparkling as she whirled around, her long, brown curls bouncing with each movement. "Someday I'm gonna be a famous dancer and have a hundred pretty dresses," she said. "I want to learn to play the piano." She tapped her fingers on a nearby table.

She drew closer to me and whispered, "I have a boyfriend. He's really cute."

"You have a pretty name," I said finally. Emma was beginning to remind me of Joan, all bubbly and chatty. "My name is Beatrice. I like kittens. I wanna own lots of cats . . . and horses . . . when I grow up. My cousins have kittens on their farm."

"I found a kitten once," Emma went on, sitting on the floor next to my chair. "He was hiding under our porch. My mom said I couldn't keep him. He liked to jump straight up like this." She curled her fingers and jerked them into the air. "He ran around the house, up and down curtains and under furniture. We could hardly ever catch him."

I stared into space before speaking again. "I have a big sister. Her name is Joan. She was teaching me to read. She didn't come here with me. I don't know where she is." I looked around the room. "I hate it here. That big sister threw away my brand new dress. What is this place? Who are all those sisters?"

Emma sprang up and put her hands on her hips, her mouth open in disbelief. She shook her head. "This is an orphanage. St. Joe's. Didn't anybody tell you that?"

I shook my head.

Emma chattered on. "The sisters? The one you came in with is Sister Edythe. You gotta look out for her. She watches you to see if you're doing anything bad. You never know when she'll sneak up behind you. She'll be sure to report you to Sister Agatha. She's the Sister Superior.

"The nun over there," Emma pointed to the group playing the board game. "She's Sister Rose. She takes care of the big girls. She can play any game. She'll play with you if you ask her. The one in the dining room is Sister Nathan. She's okay. There's a lot more nuns. You'll get to see most of 'em."

Emma pointed to a table by the windows and told me to sit there. "I'll go get my book of paper dolls. They're in that cupboard over there by the wall. Everyone has their own cubbyhole. You'll get one," she stated. When she returned, she opened the book and took out three cardboard figures of shapely girls in one-piece swimsuits. She spread the remainder of the book's contents on the table. We sorted through the dresses and fancy gowns, slacks and blouses, swimsuits and shorts, and attached them to the dolls with tabs at their shoulders and waists.

"Don't you wish you could go home?" I asked suddenly.

"I can't," Emma said. "My mom died, and I don't know where my father is. My two brothers are in a foster home."

"Will you go with them?"

"No, they just wanted boys. It's a farm. How many brothers and sisters do you have?"

When I hesitated, Emma didn't wait for an answer. "That's okay. You don't have to tell me. A lot of kids don't talk about family stuff. I guess that's because they're sad."

At 7:00 p.m., Sister Edythe reentered the playroom and took a small bell from her wide sleeve. As the bell tinkled, some of the girls scrambled to stow their playthings and gathered near the door. Emma ran to jam her book of cutouts into its compartment and raced to my side.

"The big girls stay up until eight o'clock," she breathed. "We hafta go to bed now."

I stayed behind Emma as Sister Edythe led us single file up to the third-floor dormitories. "The big girls get this end," Emma said with a flourish of her hand.

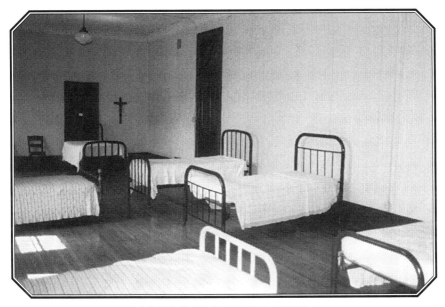

Third-floor dorm, July, 1978
Courtesy of the Diocese of Green Bay Archives

A peek into a passing bathroom reminded me of the recent scrubbing. Emma stuck her head in another room flanked by rows of metal lockers. "The middle girls sleep here," she said. "They also have a bigger room across the hall.

"That's where we sleep," she pointed to the hall's south end. "The Wardrobe is over there."

I turned around to see where she was pointing. "What's in there?" I asked.

"That's where we get our clothes," she answered.

When Emma attempted to say more, Sister Edythe silenced her with a wave of her hand. Pulling me down beside her, we joined the other girls kneeling on the corridor's wooden floor for evening prayers. After the last amen was spoken, the girls dispersed to their lockers and dorm rooms. When Emma tried to give me more bedtime instructions, Sister Edythe cut her off and told me to come with her.

The nun first showed me the central bathroom. Whitewashed, the windowless room had eighteen sinks back-to-back down the center with lavatories at both ends. Girls were in their underwear; some were washing themselves, others were brushing their teeth.

Sister Edythe next led me to the row of lockers. In a slot near the top of the one she opened was a tag marked "B4." Inside, neatly folded on the top shelf, was a pair of pajamas. Sister Edythe told me I'd get the rest of my clothes the next day. She beckoned me to follow her and led the way to one of the two rooms reserved for the youngest girls.

The twelve beds in the room were iron-painted white. Three girls sitting on one scattered when they saw Sister Edythe. Another girl pulled pajamas from under a pillow. When she saw Sister Edythe, she tried to hide them behind her. The nun reminded her that all her clothes belonged in her locker.

Sister Edythe showed me to a bed and told me this was where I would sleep. Rolling the bedspread into even folds to the bed's foot, she added, "When you are done changing, hang your dress in your locker."

"Lights out at seven thirty sharp," the nun called out and left the room.

Hanging up my dress, I took the pajamas from the shelf. Inside the pajamas was a tag labeled "B4." I put them on. The soft fabric felt good next to my skin.

Back in the dorm room, I walked over to the bed that was going to be mine. *A bed all my own!* I lifted the pillow which revealed five inches of stiffly pressed sheet folded over the blanket. I pulled back the blanket and was surprised to see another sheet under the one that was folded over the blanket. *Two sheets? On one bed?* Pulling away one of the corners of the sheet, I felt the stiff rubber mattress pad underneath.

The room was hot and muggy. I walked to a set of double windows, hoping to catch a breeze from the stately trees out front, but the windows were closed and wouldn't budge. Distant car headlights winked through the silent leaves. People entered a small building by the river.

More girls came into the room; Emma was not among them. I climbed into bed and slipped my arms between the sheets as the bell sounded. I lay in the dark, feeling lonelier than I had ever felt in my young life. I couldn't believe what had happened to me that day: the ride to Green Bay, Ellen's leaving me behind, the rough way Sister Edythe handled me. The only bright spot was meeting Emma.

I thought about my brothers and sisters. Would I ever see them again? Would I ever go home? What about Joan? Where was she? Joan was the center of my universe, my teacher, my best friend.

I was sure I could not survive without my nine-year-old sister. I drifted into a restless sleep. My dreams were fitful and disjointed: black cars, fields and horses, castles and courtrooms, haystacks and kittens. My siblings drifted in and out. Joan was reaching for me.

I awoke, half-conscious. *Was it just a bad dream?* The darkness obscured all sensibilities. I drifted out again.

CHAPTER THREE

September 1942 – March 1943
The Orphanage
Abandoned

Iawakened to the sound of a bell, sleepy and confused. *Where am I?* Then
I remembered everything that happened the previous day. The memory
hit me like a slap. So did my wet pajama bottoms. I was afraid to get up.
I had wet the bed. I couldn't recall the last time that happened at home.
Then Joan had helped me clean up and get into dry clothes before my
mother found out. Not that Glenda would have cared; she didn't seem to
notice things like wet pajamas or beds. But Sister Edythe probably would.

Most of my roommates had left the dorm room before the nun came
in. I slid out of bed and flipped the sheet and blanket over the pillow. Sister
Edythe pulled them back to the end of the bed. The knots in my stomach
tightened.

"Come for morning prayers," the nun said. She directed me in front of
where the girls were already kneeling. A couple girls snickered. I suddenly
realized they could see my wet bottoms. I blushed with embarrassment.

After prayers, Sister Edythe told me to wash up, get dressed, and leave
my wet things on the bed. She'd get someone to help me with them later.
Most of the other girls had already made their beds and were lining up in the
corridor. Emma squeezed in next to me and told me we were going to Mass.

The chapel was one flight down. The nuns were already there, occupying
two rows in the back. Boys entered from the north side, girls from the
south. Kneelers dropped, some with loud bangs, and everyone knelt. A gong
sounded. A priest and two altar boys entered the sanctuary and walked to the
front of the altar. They bowed, and Mass began.

Second floor, Chapel
Courtesy of the Diocese of Green Bay Archives

I paid little attention to the liturgy. I was fascinated by the beauty of the chapel, the round arches, the lighted altar area with candles and statues. I turned to look up at the choir loft with its organ and rows of wooden chairs, but I saw Sister Edythe frowning at me. I turned around and tried to focus on the service.

During the half-hour break before breakfast, some of the kids rushed to perform chores, dusting, mopping, and polishing sinks. Those with unmade beds hurried to make them before Sister Edythe wrote them up for demerits. Some of the girls had taken the down stairs on the way out of chapel. I saw them later in the dining room helping Sister Nathan dish up breakfast, an almost colorless mush, buttered whole wheat bread, and milk. After everyone had filed in and was seated, the tinkling bell sounded and we said Grace.

"Bless us, O Lord . . . "

Prayer was followed by the energetic clanging of tin utensils against heavy chinaware. At the bell's next tinkling, the room erupted in noisy prattle. Minutes later, another bell and it stopped. After the last few minutes of silence, we said closing Grace.

"We give you thanks . . . " And silence.

Once again, I refused to eat. *I'll starve myself; that'll show 'em*, I sulked.

Emma gave me a sympathetic look on her way out of the dining room. When Sister Rose, the morning's lone supervisor, saw how distraught I was, she walked over to me, smiled and said, "It's okay, you can leave."

Back in the dorm, I had to face a disgruntled Sister Edythe. The nun assigned Laura, an older girl, to change my bed and take the wet sheets over to Melania (the laundry). I watched Laura in silence, chastened by Sister Edythe's rebuke, "Don't let it happen again."

Softening her tone, Sister Edythe beckoned, "Come with me."

Scraping my feet and crinkling my nose, I followed Sister into the Wardrobe. Just as I was preparing to hate Sister Edythe forever, the nun redeemed herself, albeit temporarily. Stopping at a rack of dresses, the nun told me I could pick two. I selected a plain blue that reminded me of the one she had trashed. The second one caught my eye because it was covered with flowers—some blue—on a white background.

When Sister Edythe held a light blue pleated skirt up to my waist, I thought I might have misjudged the nun. She seemed to understand my passion for blue. *Maybe the Sister wasn't so bad after all.*

Next, Sister Edythe handed me a white blouse and a cream-colored cardigan to go with the skirt. She completed my wardrobe with three pairs of anklets, two pairs of thick tan stockings, two underpants, and a pair of pajamas.

At noon, I considered again the possibility of liking Sister Edythe when she let me off after I pushed away my plate of pork 'n' beans and bologna. I was sticking to my plan to starve myself.

But at supper that evening, Sister Edythe had had enough. She told me I couldn't leave the table until I ate all my food. She was prepared to stay no matter how long it took.

The soup looked as unappetizing as the mush from breakfast, only grayer. I was sure I would throw up if I ate it. Sister's frown and lips pressed into a thin line convinced me otherwise. I forced down the now-cold soup and ran from the room.

A week later I wet the bed again. Again I was made to kneel, humiliated, in front of the girls. At the noon meal, Sister Edythe read the names of the bedwetters. As punishment, wormwood, a bitter herb in liquid form, was poured over the offenders' food.

I took a forkful of the tainted food and raised it to my lips, but that's as far as it got. I didn't care what Sister Edythe would do to me. *I'll be here forever,* I told myself, *because I can't eat this.*

I was trying hard not to cry when I noticed a boy at the next table waving his hand, trying to get my attention. He lowered his head and spoke as loudly as he dared. "I'll take your plate, you can have mine."

Another boy helped by diverting Sister Edythe's attention. He pinched a girl at his table. As the girl squealed, the plates were exchanged. The first boy ate my food without grimacing. He glanced my way, a silly grin on his face. I returned his smile, but I never discovered the reason for his kindness. Maybe he had a crush on me; maybe that was what boys at the orphanage did for girls. I liked to think that maybe he understood what I was going through.

Each day brought the same humdrum existence: up early every morning, attend Mass, do chores, and stay out of Sister Edythe's way. I'd managed not to wet the bed again. Other than Emma, I made few close friends. I was sure that any day someone was going to come and take me home.

Six months after my arrival at the orphanage, in early 1943, I was ordered to report to Sister Agatha's office, a room I had passed often on the way to my classes—school had started shortly after my arrival. *Oh, oh, what did I do?* I couldn't remember doing anything bad enough to be sent to the Sister Superior's office, at least not anything I got caught at. Then I thought maybe the summons could mean good news. Maybe it was about Joan. Maybe it meant the day I had waited and prayed for had come. Maybe it meant I could go home.

When I entered Sister Agatha's office, the nun was seated at a wooden desk. In front of the desk were two straight back chairs, and I seated myself in one of them. The nun opened a folder in front of her.

She got right to the point. "Your parents are getting a divorce," she stated noncommittally. As she spoke, I could feel the blood drain from my face. "The judge has declared your mother unfit to care for you."

My heart leaped into my throat. I'm sure I stopped breathing. Sister Agatha didn't take notice of my distress. She continued. "There are no suitable foster homes available. You will stay here for now."

"You mean I can't go home?"

"That's right," the nun answered.

"What about my sister?"

Sister Agatha closed the folder and stood up.

"Why can't I go home? Where's my sister?"

"There is nothing more I can tell you."

I knew by the nun's stony face that I would get no more information. All I wanted was to get away and be alone in my misery.

I ran up the two flights of stairs to my dorm room and dropped to the floor beside my bed. My eyes rained tears. I pictured Joan reading to me, teaching me words that she had just learned. I missed her hugs.

Suddenly I realized that Sister Agatha hadn't mentioned my younger sister and brothers. *Were they still at home? Where was my mother now?*

I sobbed until there were no more tears.

When there was no further word about Joan in the weeks and months ahead, I knew I would have to learn to survive without my sister. The hard shell that would surround me most of my life had started to form.

CHAPTER FOUR

1944
The Orphanage
Unwelcome Visitors

T he only break that occurred in the silence regarding my family happened nearly a year later.

Sundays were visiting days at the orphanage. Relatives were welcomed for two hours in the auditorium after the 1:00 p.m. Benediction service. Whether or not we expected company, we had to spend the time in our classrooms. One of the kids, acting as a runner, came to the classroom and called out the names of those who had visitors. Those whose names were not called stayed in the classroom reading, writing letters to family, napping, or goofing off. Those who chose the last activity had to avoid the monitor, often a "teacher's pet," who enjoyed his or her newfound power to write up detention slips.

One Sunday the runner called my name. I jumped up, excited. *"Who'd visit me?"* When I got to the auditorium, I stared in disbelief. There sat my mother and father. I was torn between greeting them and hightailing it back to the classroom.

I hadn't seen my mother since before coming to St. Joe's. I remembered little of my father and wondered why he had even come. Weren't my parents supposed to be divorced?

I ignored my father, exchanged an awkward hug with my mother. Glenda reached into a bag on the floor and handed me a package.

"Open it," she said. "I had to guess how big you'd be."

Just then, I noticed a boy and girl standing in the auditorium doorway. I didn't recognize my brother Joe and sister Ann at first; I hadn't seen them in more than a year and a half. I was dumbfounded. I wondered where they had come from.

Glenda beckoned the youngsters to her. No one spoke. When she tried to start a conversation, Joe stood with his arms dangling at his sides. Ann covered her face with one small hand.

"Where have you been all this time?" I asked my siblings.

When they didn't say anything, I turned to Glenda and demanded, "Do you know where they've been?"

"I thought you knew," Glenda said, her voice low. "They were brought here right after you."

"Then why haven't I seen them?" I asked. "Where are Frank and Edward? And where's Joan?" The last question was asked through tears.

My mother fumbled with explanations. The four younger children were picked up the next day. Ann and Joe went to the orphanage nursery (Nazareth Hall), Frank and Edward, to a foster home.

"What about Joan?" I stared at my mother.

"I can't tell you anything about her."

While families around us talked and laughed, mine barely looked at each other. When visiting hours were over at 4:00 p.m., Glenda promised to write. I watched as a nun I hadn't seen before escorted my brother and sister away.

Later in my dorm room, I found a sky-blue taffeta dress inside the package my mother had brought. I remembered another new blue dress my mother had gotten for me and what had happened to that one. I stuffed the dress inside my nightstand.

My mother wrote a few letters. In one she told me she had moved to Chicago. There was never news about my father. After a while the letters stopped.

Later that year, after Joe turned six, he was moved to the main orphanage building. Ann followed in 1945. Although I saw them occasionally, I didn't know how to act like a sister. We'd never had a chance to bond. I'd have to say I didn't feel anything. I don't remember much about my family life other than Joan and my cousins. Here at the orphanage, we were a number, one among many. Younger children were kept separate from the older ones, the youngest in a separate building. My two youngest brothers, Frank and Edward, were in a foster home. I never saw them.

I felt I had no family, that I was truly an orphan.

CHAPTER FIVE

April 1942
Northeastern Wisconsin
Home

I rolled over on the lumpy mattress in the bed I shared with my two sisters. Ann, a tiny, blue-eyed blonde, not yet three, was asleep. Eight-year-old Joan was already up and dressed. I watched Joan ruffle her thick, brown hair as she walked toward the bed, smiling at me.

Our mother, Glenda, was in bed. Our dad, Harold, stumbled around in the bathroom. Next door to our room, three-and-a-half-year-old Joe and eighteen-month-old Frank were asleep.

Joan helped me with my dress and kissed the small round face looking up at her. Hand-in-hand we strolled to the boys' bedroom. The stink coming from that room sent me fleeing for the stairs of the two-story house on Third Street where we'd moved after our family had grown to five—that was two babies ago. She dressed the boys and, carrying Frank, hurried past the bathroom. There was no way for me to know then how uneasy she was whenever she confronted Harold, the man who seemed to have an aversion to his oldest daughter. That if he paid any attention to her at all, it was only to criticize.

After feeding the crew, Joan tidied up the kitchen, and waited for our father to leave before going upstairs to gather the dirty laundry. She'd help our mother with it after school.

My mother had a hard time keeping track of me. She let me go to the park across the street alone, but with strict instructions not to go any farther. My rebellious streak was already exerting itself, and I liked to go exploring. When I wandered too far into unfamiliar territory, I'd look around for a policeman to take me home. One time an officer found me huddled under a tree in a thunderstorm. When he asked me what I was doing there, I informed him that "I was just waiting for the thunder to stop."

One April afternoon in 1942, the park did not hold enough adventure for me. I went looking for more in the garage behind the house. It was filled with junk left over from our last move: broken furniture, old tools, and a hodgepodge of boxes, the contents of some spilling out on the garage's dirt floor.

When I could find nothing to interest me in the boxes, I turned my attention to a tire sitting high up on the edge of an old mattress. I tried to climb up to the tire but lost my footing. I reached out for the mattress, but there was nothing to hold onto. I fell, hitting the left side of my head, gashing it open.

My screams brought Glenda running. She carried me into the house and wrapped a towel around my head. A neighbor woman, hearing the commotion, phoned the police. She stayed with my younger siblings while the officer took my mother and me to the hospital.

The cut required several stitches. The doctor covered my head with a gauze bandage and assured my mother that the wound would heal nicely. He told Glenda to return with me in ten days to have the stitches removed. The nurse helping the doctor gave me a sucker. After interviewing the physician for his report, the policeman took us home.

Joan, coming from school and seeing the patrol car in front of the house, rushed inside to find out what was going on. She found me wearing my bandage as though it were a royal crown and licking on my sucker. Joan caressed my face and burst into tears.

"Don't cry," I said. "Look what I got." I held up the sucker. "And I got to ride in a police car!"

Joan sank into the sofa next to me. "Does it hurt?"

"Yeah. They sewed my head up with a needle."

Joan hugged me again. "I'm sorry I wasn't here to protect you."

"You'd better let her rest," Glenda interrupted.

CHAPTER SIX

1930s
Northeastern Wisconsin
Not So Sweet

G lenda was a wild one. The second oldest of five children, she hadn't had an easy life, although she wasn't doing much to help herself. Her mother died when she was sixteen. Glenda left home to escape an abusive father.

In 1932, at age twenty, she found herself pregnant. She went for pregnancy counseling in April of 1933 when she was seven months pregnant. After that, she moved into St. Mary's Mothers and Infants' Home, a home for unwed mothers in Green Bay, where Joan was born. Glenda was going to put Joan up for adoption but changed her mind and stayed at St. Mary's with Joan until November of 1933. She was only required to nurse her baby for three months but stayed five and a half months before moving in with her sister Alice and brother-in-law Matt.

The house was small for two families; Alice and Matt already had three children. Alice wanted Glenda to move out. Matt thought Glenda should have a husband. He knew just the man: Harold, a bachelor Matt worked with at the paper mill. One day he took Harold aside and told him about his sister-in-law. Harold, fifteen years older than Glenda, agreed to meet her.

The couple was married in 1934 when Joan was a year old. Glenda was sure that her new husband would offer her a stable lifestyle.

It was the Depression. Times were tough and getting tougher. Harold woke up every morning never knowing if he had a job. Glenda and Harold lost their first child, a boy born prematurely at eight months. He lived only a month.

I was born in 1935. Two babies followed, a girl and a boy, both born prematurely, each dying within a day. The next four years brought four more babies, all of whom survived.

As the family grew, Glenda's life began to spiral out of control. She couldn't handle the pressure of a large family, and when Harold broke his hand and was laid off from his job, things only got worse. Instead of helping her around the house, he stayed away until the cigarettes and beer ran out. When he was home, he locked himself in the boys' bedroom and listened to the radio. Sometimes he watched a neighborhood baseball game in the park across the street from the upstairs window.

Though this was the atmosphere that my brothers and sisters and I grew up in, at the time I was not aware of the serious problems within our family.

CHAPTER SEVEN

The Middle of August 1942
Northeastern Wisconsin
No Goodbyes

"C'mon, lazybones, time to get up."

Joan traced tickley fingers across my naked back. I rolled over to the familiar voice. Because school hadn't yet begun, Joan lingered around the house. She had become a mother hen after my fall.

"You're going to Uncle Matt's for a few days."

"Yeaaaaaaa. Are you coming with us?"

"No, Mother needs me to stay home," Joan said. "I told her I'm old enough to take care of Dad."

Again, had I known the situation between Joan and my father, I would have been surprised that she wanted to stay home with him. It was many years later that I learned the real reason.

Joan had no intention of staying home, not with Harold in the house. She had plenty of friends who would take her in. The problem was she didn't like going to the farm; she felt uncomfortable there.

I, however, could not conceal my excitement. A stay at Aunt Alice and Uncle Matt's farm meant running wild with my cousins and relishing Aunt Alice's cookies.

After the twenty-minute trip into the country and chores out of the way, my cousins, Darrel and Jane, and I set out to do whatever five and six-year-olds could find to do without getting into too much trouble. Running through the fields, exploring in and around the barn, climbing up and sliding down haystacks qualified. Trying to catch chickens came in last. After relentlessly pursuing the pesky fowl, I was forced to retreat when an enormous rooster mistook my bare toes for kernels of corn. I had to run fast to get out of his way. I decided kittens were more preferable; they were soft and furry and not particularly fond of toes. Earlier, I had spotted a box with a momma and lots of babies. I picked up a gray one with four white paws and put it up to my ear so I could hear the soft purring as it struggled to get free. I knelt by the box, petting the kittens, hoping these would be spared. I had watched, horrified, one day at the farm while my uncle drowned a whole litter in a pail of water.

On the third morning, Aunt Alice rounded up my meager belongings. Cupping my face in her hands she said, "Young lady, you are going home today, but the others are staying for a few more days. I packed you some cookies and a dress of Jane's."

My uncle boosted me into the truck for the ride home. As soon as it came to a stop, I climbed down and ran into the house. "Joan," I called out, "I'm home."

Joan came downstairs. "Come and see your new baby brother. His name is Edward."

I had been so excited about my trip to the country, and now with my new baby brother, I failed to notice that Joan was not her normal happy self.

The next day my mother was upstairs nursing Edward. She had sent Joan to the drug store for a few baby items. Joe, Ann, and Frank were still at the farm. I sat cross-legged on the living room sofa counting pinecones Joan had helped me gather from the park.

"Don't move from that couch until Joan gets back, and don't answer the door for anyone," my mother had instructed.

I could tell by her tone that she meant business. When there was a knock on the door, I leaned forward. From my vantage point, I couldn't see who it was, but I didn't get up.

"Hello, anyone home?" a woman's voice called out.

My mother came downstairs carrying Edward and stood close to the screen door. I was a few feet away so I could hear them.

"I just got home with the baby yesterday," my mother said. "Can't this wait?"

"I must talk to you." The woman's voice was pleasant.

I wiggled into the sofa while my mother vented.

"I've had all the talk I want. I'm not talking to anyone anymore."

"I'm trying to help you," the woman replied.

My mother said, "Well, you know what you can do with your help."

"Please," the woman said. "I'll only take a few minutes of your time."

My mother relented and opened the door. "Let me put the baby to bed," she said.

I tilted my head to see the woman, who I later learned was a caseworker, walking through the living room. She wore a dark suit and carried a brown, leather case.

In 1930, the Green Bay Diocese Apostolate became the coordinating agency for child welfare services. Caseworkers, some of them volunteers, worked with local courts in cases where dependent and neglected Catholic children were involved. Ellen Johnson was assigned to my family's case.

"Hi, my name is Ellen," she said to me. "You must be Beatrice."

I stared at her and turned my attention once again to my pinecones.

The two women went into the kitchen. I could hear them talking but could not make out what they were saying. Joan's name was mentioned several times.

As Ellen was leaving, my mother screamed at her, "They're not going to take my children away from me. I'll kill them first."

I covered my head with a quilt my mother kept on the sofa. I didn't want to hear anymore.

About a week later, Ellen came to our house again. My mother refused to let her in. Ellen told my mother that I had to testify at a hearing on Monday, August 31.

"I'll be here to pick her up at two o'clock," Ellen said through the screen door.

My mother didn't say anything, and Ellen left.

"What's a hearing?" I asked my mother. "And what's testify mean?"

"Nothing," she said. "Nothing for you to worry about."

But just the way she said it, I knew I had something to worry about. *Why doesn't my mother ever tell me anything? Why does she treat me like a baby?*

When Ellen and I arrived at the Outagamie County Courthouse for the hearing, Ellen told me that a judge wanted to talk to me and that he would expect me to answer his questions truthfully.

"I'll be nearby if you need me," Ellen said, trying to calm me.

"Is Joan here?" I asked.

"No, honey. She's going to talk to the judge later."

"Oh . . . Where is she now?"

Before Ellen could come up with an answer, a door opened and we were called in. Ellen helped me into a chair in the front of the room and sat down next to me. I looked around for my mother but didn't see her. The courtroom was empty except for the judge. I inched closer to Ellen.

"Miss Johnson." The judge motioned for Ellen to bring me forward.

"Good morning, Beatrice," he said after I was seated in a chair at the front of the courtroom.

I stared at the man towering above me.

"Do you know why you're here?" the judge asked.

"Ellen said you're gonna ask me some questions."

The judge paused for a moment before continuing.

"Are you happy at home?"

I hesitated, then answered softly.

"Yes."

"What do you do at home?

"My sister reads to me and we play with her doll."

"Is that all you do?" the judge asked.

"We go to the park."

"Do you go to the park often?"

"Not much anymore."

"Why is that?"

"My mother said I can't go unless Joan is with me."

"Do you know why?"

"No."

The judge turned in his chair to face me. "I understand you fell and cut your head earlier this summer. Is that right?"

"Yes."

"What happened?"

"I was in the garage and fell down."

"Was anyone with you?"

"No."

"Where was your mother?"

"In the house."

The judge shifted his position and flipped through the pages. "How often is your father home?"

"I don't know."

"Do you see him every day?"

"No, not every day."

"Do you know where he was when you fell?"

"I think he was at work."

The judge paused again, continuing a few moments later.

"The first time Ellen came to your house, was anyone else in the house, other than you and your mother?"

"My baby brother, Edward; we call him Eddy."

"Do you know what Ellen and your mother talked about?"

"No. I couldn't hear them."

"Do you remember what your mother said before Ellen left?"

He read out loud. "'They're not going to take my children away from me. I'll kill them first.' Is that what your mother said?"

The judge turned to face me. I looked over at Ellen, then the floor, and answered, "Yes."

My siblings and I were remanded to the Green Bay Catholic Diocese Apostolate to determine the best course of action for each of us. I was brought to St. Joseph's Orphanage on Thursday, September 3, 1942. I didn't know then what happened to my younger sister and brothers or that Joan had been at the orphanage only two nights before in a bedroom on the second floor.

CHAPTER EIGHT

The Orphanage
Living and Learning

Early on, I realized that I would have to yield to the daily routine at the orphanage where the intrusive sound of bells dictated our every move. The bells woke us, called us to prayers and school, and silenced us at meals. But there were other times we couldn't talk, after lights out at bedtime, for instance, and there were severe consequences for disobedience.

We were forever standing in lines, upstairs, downstairs, in hallways. And there were so many rules to remember. "Stay next to the wall," Sister would say. "Don't touch the wall. Don't ever touch a nun or sass a nun."

We weren't allowed to show our feelings. We worked, we prayed, we studied, we slept, a timetable that left not much time for play. It was almost as if we were nuns in training.

Over in the nursery, with its ramps, floors of cork, and baby toilets, there weren't so many rules. During the day, preschoolers and babies played in a playroom decorated with brightly colored tiles, some depicting animals. Everything was in miniature: a teeter-totter, wagons, tricycles, and there were dolls neatly lined up on open cupboards. The dining room contained small tables covered with green-and-white tablecloths, with benches instead of chairs. At night, the youngsters slept in green, metal cribs. No pillows or stuffed animals.

A well-run day care, you might suggest. However, at the end of the day the little ones had no one to pick them up and take them home, hug them, wipe away tears. How do you keep more than fifty children, babies some of them, all in one room, quiet for the night? The nun in charge would turn to the large wooden music box—donated to the orphanage by a priest—hoping to lull the children to sleep with its delicate tinkling sound.

The music box in Nazareth Hall
Photographs courtesy of Rita Brault

School was a bright spot for me throughout my years at St. Joe's. I found solace in my classes and in reading.

The School Sisters of Notre Dame taught grades one through eight in classrooms located on the first and second floors. There were also courses in printing for sixth-grade boys and farming for seventh and eighth graders. Sister Amanda, who was in charge of the Wardrobe, taught the older girls to sew.

The classrooms were cheerful places with tall, airy windows. Brightly colored cutouts topped blackboards, and bulletin boards displayed maps and progress charts. Each room had twenty to thirty desks. The eighth grade had an aquarium for guppies and angelfish. Two classrooms had radios

Second floor classroom, July, 1978
Courtesy of the Diocese of Green Bay Archives

During the regular school year, September to June, classes met weekdays 8:45 to 11:45 mornings, and 1:15 to 3:30 afternoons. Evening study periods were scheduled for fifth through eighth graders. There was also a six-week summer school of half-day classes.

Workshop, summer school, July, 1944
Courtesy of the Neville Public Museum of Brown County

One of my teachers had a musical sounding name and a nice smile. She'd walk up and down classroom aisles stopping to talk to her students. I remember being happy when she paused by my desk.

Another was Sister Dominica, whom I would describe as "solemn." Her words inspired me and sometimes drew me from my shell. "Be creative. Recognize your potential. Knowledge is all."

I loved being in school, learning new things. Away from the classroom, I was inclined to return to my shell when classmates made fun of me, calling me a "know-it-all."

I responded by calling my detractors "stupid." One of my teachers, hearing that response, wrote on my report card, "Beatrice must learn to consider the feelings of others."

One of the boys, who liked to torment anyone who studied hard, got his just reward from Sister Margaret, the third grade teacher. That nun kept a ruler on her desk as a reminder for the unruly or those unwilling or unable to do their lessons. One day she called the boy, a determined slacker, to the front of the class.

"Hold out your hand," Sister Margaret said. As the ruler came close to his knuckles, he jerked his hand away and hid it behind him.

"Leave your hand out," the nun repeated.

"Well, if I do, you'll hit it," he said.

Sister had other means for keeping us in line: being hit with the ruler on your legs, sometimes leaving bruises; being bopped on the head with a book. If you didn't stand up straight, you could get Sister's nails digging in your neck.

The orphanage curriculum emphasized reading. We learned using the "Dick and Jane" readers. I soon grew bored with those, and sought out other kinds of books in the library. My preference was, and is, biographies.

We were all encouraged to use the library. Its two rooms were located across from Sister Superior's office. Tables were provided for readers, or we could withdraw books. The library provided materials for classroom use.

Some of my favorite books as a young girl were about animals and their antics, like those by Beatrix Potter. Because I loved horses, I read *Black Beauty, My Friend Flicka*, and *National Velvet* (my favorite). I enjoyed fairy tales, but preferred stories about real people, such as Abigail Adams and Abraham Lincoln. Reading about people who had lived, and had done wonderful things, made me feel like I could do wonderful things too.

Religion class, with its Baltimore Catechism, was, for me at least, merely an exercise in memorization and recitation. Once a week Father John, the orphanage director, instructed the children in religion. All the girls had a crush on Father John. He livened up the classes by interacting with us and telling us stories about the saints. I imagined myself walking in a garden with St. Francis of Assisi feeding the birds and animals. The most memorable stories he told were about young children who had died and were now saints in heaven. I preferred to picture them alive and forever young, skipping happily through heavenly clouds with the angels.

Reading fed my fantasies. I was good at pretending; anything to get outside of who I was and where I was. Many times my fantasies revolved around simple dreams. In one recurrent dream, I'm walking in a grassy field when I come to a door. As I approach the door, it opens to a bright circular light. I see someone tucking a little girl in bed. That someone hugs the little girl, tells her she loves her and that she is beautiful.

Some of my night dreams, and daydreams, were frightening. Did the other girls have similar dreams? Did big, black cars come to their houses one day and carry them away? Were they as scared as I was as they passed through those heavy wooden doors from sunshine to darkness, to the care of these strange silent creatures called nuns? Did they have caring families somewhere, or were they alone like me?

Our physical needs were attended to at the orphanage. The medical care we received was adequate: checkups, dental care, and all the appropriate vaccinations. There was a room on the upper level of Melania Hall used as an infirmary for sick kids when they had to be isolated. One of the sisters, a nurse, attended to their needs. I remember the chocolate iodine tablets we got once a week.

Out with the tonsils. Nobody got to keep them. All I remember about my tonsil episode is that it's my eighth birthday and I'm standing all alone in a hallway outside the operating room in the hospital waiting my turn. Then someone takes me into the operating room, helps me climb up on what looks like a long table, and puts a mask over my face. It feels like someone is slamming a hammer in my brain, and then nothing. Afterward it's all about ice cream.

And no chores for a few days.

CHAPTER NINE

The Orphanage
A Real Workout

All the children at the orphanage, except those in the nursery, had daily chores to perform. Six and seven-year-olds were given light duties, such as dusting and sweeping the playrooms. Jobs were rotated twice a year, generally in spring and fall. We'd assemble in the auditorium for Sister Superior to announce the changes. During my eight years at St Joe's, I served in nearly all of them, some of them more than once.

The first time I was assigned to the dining room I was eight years old. Crews of ten or twelve kids worked three times a day with Sister Nathan. Boys ran the dishwashers, girls stacked the clean dishes on shelves and set the tables. We swept the floors after every meal and scrubbed them on hands and knees once a week. We were expected to do our jobs and mind our own business. Sister Nathan knew when someone was loafing. If someone snitched on the loafer, she told that person not to be a tattletale.

Working in the bungalow, where the orphanage director lived, was one of my worst jobs, but not because of the work. I was nine at the time. The residence was located northwest of the main building and ruled over by Sister Madeline. When I met Sister Madeline for the first time, I figured she had to be the sourest woman alive. That nun was just plain grumpy. She rarely spoke and never smiled.

My job was to clean everything in the kitchen and bathroom including getting down on my knees to scrub the floors. I was a hard worker and didn't mind the work, but Sister Madeline found fault with just about everything, and when she found fault, I had to do everything over.

I became defiant and belligerent, showed up late for work, and refused to do any scrubbing on my hands and knees. Whenever I was carrying a pail of water, I deliberately dropped puddles on the floor. When Sister Madeline told me to clean up the spills, I sneered at her. When Sister's back was turned, I stuck my tongue out at her.

She caught me once with my tongue out and said she would report me. *Now I've done it. I'll be on Sister Edythe's punishment list.*

Fortunately, the report was made to Sister Agatha. I found myself assigned to Sister Muriel, the librarian and music teacher. My new job was to keep the library's two rooms in order. I couldn't believe I was being rewarded for my bad behavior. And to work in the library yet! I like to think that Sister Agatha knew I needed a change.

My steamiest assignment, at age eleven, was in the laundry, a large sunny room on the first floor of Melania Hall outfitted with two washers, two dryers, and a huge mangle. Sister Clarita supervised that operation. On Mondays and Fridays, the girls who worked in the laundry carted bags of clothing and linens to Melania from the main building and Nazareth Hall through underground tunnels. Sister Clarita helped the girls sort the laundry, and the boys managed the washers and dryers. The girls folded clothes and ironed those that needed ironing.

The mangle was staffed by four children, two for starting the sheets through the rollers and two to pull them out and fold them. Bottom sheets were laundered once a week. Top sheets were switched to the bottom and the freshly laundered bottom sheets became top sheets (no fitted sheets back then).

On Wednesdays, Sister Rose and the older girls darned socks with burned-out light bulbs, needles, and multi-stranded darning cotton. With the proper network of stitches, the spot where the hole had been never saw the light of day again.

Kitchen duty was one of my least favorite assignments. I served there for two terms: when I was ten and again when I was fourteen. Six to eight girls worked three meals a day, supervised by Sister Bernadette, who was responsible for every meal that went out of the kitchen. She made the going more pleasant with her light-hearted teasing and for sharing food with her workers—including some foods that never made it to the children's dining room.

On my first day in the kitchen, I felt dwarfed by what I saw. Everything was large and stainless steel: the counter tops, tables, and mixing bowls. It looked like a small child could fit in the largest mixing bowl. Windows lined the back wall of the kitchen.

We dished up meals in the kitchen and wheeled them into the dining room on carts. Breakfast included mushy cereals in various shades of white, yellow, and gray, sometimes fruit such as sliced oranges or bananas. For dinner, we always had vegetables, fresh or canned. Rice and potatoes were the other main staples. Sometimes we'd have meat loaf or bologna with pork 'n' beans, also some cheese and eggs. Supper consisted of cream or vegetable soups. Milk and buttered bread came with every meal. The butter was made in the orphanage's creamery and the bread baked three times a week in the bakery. That was something to relish. Fresh homemade butter on homemade bread.

Potatoes came from a farm in Antigo and were stored in a basement root cellar. The kitchen girls were responsible for keeping a ready supply of peeled potatoes on hand. Once the spuds came out of the large electric potato peeler, we plucked out the starchy eyes with a knife and plopped the finished product into large water-filled pots. When we got bored, we'd toss the potatoes from across the room to see who could make the smallest—or biggest—splash. Leftover cooked potatoes were fried and served as an afternoon snack. Mashed potatoes were reserved for Sundays and holidays.

When there was dessert, it was Jell-O or pudding. When apples were in season, Sister Bernadette made "brown betty," a confection consisting of sliced apples, bread, milk, sugar, and cinnamon, and served warm. Mmmmm.

Up until 1952, the orphanage operated as a working farm. At one time, it was rated number two in the state. The Wisconsin State Reformatory (now Green Bay Correctional Institution), just one cemetery south of the orphanage, was rated number one. There is another cemetery just north of the where the orphanage once stood. The legend back then was that orphans, inmates, and the deceased might have outnumbered the local population in this small township of Allouez, located between Green Bay and De Pere.

Farm, looking east, 1940s
Courtesy of the Neville Public Museum of Brown County

The farm was owned by the Catholic Diocese of Green Bay and run by two farmers hired from the community. The young men and their families lived in the apartments on Melania's second floor. Boys from the orphanage vied to be their helpers.

The farm included a pig barn for thirty-plus pigs and a second barn for up to forty cows. Most of the acreage was used for grain: corn, oats, and hay, such as timothy and alfalfa. Contractors cut and baled hay and butchered the livestock.

The farm also had a large chicken coop, the inhabitants of which were intended for our dinner on some Sundays and on holidays. Getting the hapless fowl from farmyard to dinner plate presented a certain hazard for everyone involved—most notably the chickens. First of all the birds had to be rendered headless—don't even want to think about how the farmers accomplished that. Next, the intermediaries, better known as the kitchen girls, took over. One crew dunked the unfortunates in pots of scalding water and passed them on to another, who furiously relieved them of their plumage. The last stop was at Sister Bernadette's station. She purged them of their nasty innards, separated them from their wings and legs, and spread them in rows in pans for the trip to the large, roasting ovens.

I abhorred the entire operation. There was the stench, of course. And, notwithstanding my toe-pecking incident at my uncle's farm, I hated seeing animals hurt in any way. Add to that my vision of the creatures happily clucking their way around the farmyard, and it was too much to bear.

Scouring endless pots and pans, washing down miles of counters, and scrubbing acres of floors was not on anybody's favorites list. Neither was rounding up wet chicken feathers. They had to be picked up by hand because they stuck to everything.

There were certain advantages to working in the kitchen, however. Some of the local bakeries donated day-old baked goods delivered in brass-colored canisters. For the swift-of-hand and stealth-of-foot, this was manna from heaven.

While much food moved in and out of the kitchen, not all of it made its way to the children's dining room. For instance, the closest we ever got to bacon was the joyful, smoky fragrance emanating from another room (there must have been a back kitchen that we didn't know about, or the sisters did their cooking during the midnight hours). The alternative was something we called greebles. Served hot or cold, the small chunks of rendered-to-a-crisp back fat could not make it past my now defunct tonsils. When served as an after school snack, I passed them up, but when they made their way to the dinner table, I was forced to pawn them off. With plenty of boys who relished the crunchy tidbit, us greeble haters had only to slide them off our plates and pass them from hand to hand under the table till they reached those connoisseurs of Epicurean delights.

Below the kitchen were two walk-in freezers and two coolers. There was also a root cellar to store potatoes, and other rooms with shelves for canned goods. Off the kitchen was a room used exclusively for separating and pasteurizing raw milk, an operation we were only allowed to watch. We'd carry the buckets of cream to the kitchen where Sister Bernadette churned the cream into butter. Then we'd press the butter in small loaf pans to be refrigerated for later use. The remaining (blue) milk was a staple of the children's diet.

The orphanage also supplied milk for the McCormick Home, a home for the elderly, managed by the Green Bay Catholic Diocese.

When the orphanage ceased to be a working farm in 1952, some of the acreage was turned into cash cropping. One of the boys did the plowing and cultivating, and planted the corn. The orphanage contracted with a local farmer who planted beans and carrots and hired crews to pick the vegetables. The boys planted tomatoes and weeded the gardens. They were paid half a cent per pound for picking vegetables. A special treat after a long hot day in the fields was a swim in the East River on the east side of Green Bay, or at Geano's beach on the bay of Green Bay in Little Suamico.

Looking west toward the Fox River, 1941
Courtesy of the Neville Public Museum of Brown County

Some jobs were more pleasant than others. In the summer, the sisters would gather bushels of peonies from the peony patch. A few chosen girls hauled the flowers in wagons to the end of the driveway by Riverside Drive and sold them for $1 a dozen. If the day was particularly warm and they got thirsty, one of the girls would take the wagon and lug buckets of water back to their shady spot under the apple trees.

I spent part of my thirteenth year engaged in one of the more pleasant jobs, working in the bakery with Sister Isabel, a round, jolly nun whose apron ties defied the laws of *girthhood*. Three days a week, we poked and punched and kneaded, to replenish the ever-depleted supply of bread which was served at every meal.

Friday evenings we scrubbed the first two floors in the main building on our hands and knees, the others we mopped. Six to twelve unsupervised kids managed to get the floors clean while playing shuffleboard with the thick cotton string mop heads and brown soap bars.

We were no strangers to hard work—or mischief.

CHAPTER TEN

The Orphanage
Monkeyshines

O n our best days, we could try even a saintly sister's patience to no end with our "whodunits." Like sneaking food out of the dining room, hiding it, and forgetting about it until it stunk up the place. Or pinching someone in chapel. Or climbing down a fire escape, when there wasn't a fire drill. The underground rule for that caper was to leave the door to the fire escape unlocked for the next perpetrator. The location of the bell tower on the third level above the chapel with stairs to the cupola and widow's peak provided ample climbing opportunities for adventuresome boys.

The girls' dormitories on the south side of the third floor and the boys' dormitories on the north side were connected by a fire door. Often at night, after lights out, one *side* would knock and wait for the other to knock back. I don't believe that door was ever unlocked—but I could be wrong.

Sometimes when the sisters were in one of their regular two-hour meetings, several of the braver girls dragged mattresses off the beds and used them to slide down the staircases. They knew they could get caught, but some adventures are worth the consequences.

To us kids, the sisters were a continual mystery. We thought of them as these omnipresent creatures with complete power over us. We had tons of questions and theories about the women religious. Were they ever ordinary people wearing street clothes? Were they allowed to take off those black habits? We assumed they did. How else would they take a bath? How could they stand the heavy black garments in the hot summer? And what did they wear underneath?

We also wondered if the nuns ever ate; we never saw them eat. They must never have dribbled on those stiff white collars they wore over their robes, mustn't they have?

Other speculation ran to how the nuns walked, or did they? They seemed to float like silent black mounds.

How many pairs of eyes did the sisters have? We caught on early that their veils deprived them of peripheral vision. They could only see anything on either side of themselves if they completely turned their heads. But they made up for that with a second set of eyes in the back of their heads that could see through anything, we believed. Like when they scolded a mischievous student in the classroom's rear while facing the blackboard.

The real puzzlement, however, was what the nuns had under those white bonnet-like coverings on their heads. "Do you think they have hair, or did they cut it all off?" was the question. We'd watch the nuns stroll the sidewalks between the orphanage and the other buildings saying their daily prayers and wonder. I never did find out.

But Evelyn, a gal who had been at the orphanage about five years after I left, did, and she shared the story with me.

One day, while she and some of her friends contemplated new ways to torment the nuns, one of them came up with an inspiration that was too good to pass up. They explained their "deliciously evil" plot to other girls who had had run-ins with Sister Edythe.

At that time, the kids' dorms were in the new residence building, Bona Hall. Sister Edythe's bedroom was adjacent to one of the dorm rooms. The two rooms were connected by a small sliding door at the top which could only be opened from the nun's side.

The girls figured Sister Edythe slept without her veil. How could she sleep if she left it on? If they created a rumpus, she wouldn't have time to grab the veil before she investigated what was happening. They had gotten one of the boys who worked with an orphanage handyman to loan them a flashlight.

On the night designated for the conspiracy to take place, the girls went about their normal business, didn't want to bring any undue attention to themselves. After they had retired, assured that they were all sleeping, Sister

Edythe went to her room. The girls heard the door close and later the squeak of her bedsprings as she lay down.

"Now," hissed Evelyn. They jumped from their beds and pounded their feet on the floor. Some of them clapped hands. Others clanged the rails on their iron beds with spoons confiscated from the dining room. Then they jumped back into bed.

They heard a *click* as Sister Edythe opened the partition. Out came the flashlight, catching the nun in the face. She covered her eyes with the back of her hand.

Somebody whispered, "She does have hair."

Sister Edythe slammed the sliding door shut. "We had a hard time keeping our giggles quiet." Evelyn giggled as she said it.

The next day nothing was said. As the girls knelt in the corridor for morning prayers, a few of them looked at Sister Edythe and snickered. A cold look from the nun silenced them.

Although they talked about the nun's "unveiling" for days, Sister Edythe never reported the miscreants. She did not retaliate with punishments.

While we kids did our best to break all the rules, the nuns were equally vigilant in their efforts to see that we obeyed them. I think it was a draw.

CHAPTER ELEVEN

The Orphanage
Holidays

Every March 19th, we celebrated the feast of St. Joseph. The day started out with a High Mass, school was suspended for the day, and only necessary kitchen and dining room chores had to be done. The holiday spirit spilled over into the playrooms and the playground with competitive games like ring toss. Candy and trinkets were the prizes.

Easter Sunday was the grand culmination of all the days that came before it, starting with Lent and its forty days of penance. We attended the Stations of the Cross every Friday. During Holy Week, we practically lived in church. Holy Thursday meant a twenty-four-hour vigil of prayer and meditation. All of us in grades three and up participated. Good Friday services began at noon and ended at 3:00 p.m.

Those of us assigned to the bakery helped Sister Isabel frost hot cross buns with white frosting crosses. We watched her create bunny cakes using bunny-shaped pans, and then loading them up with fluffy frosting and coconut. The cakes were displayed in the dining room during Easter Week, and after that, they disappeared. I don't recall anyone ever solving the mystery of where they went.

Lent officially ended at noon on Easter Saturday, and we turned our thoughts to spring and warm weather, shedding our thick tan stockings for the lighter anklets, new dresses, and Easter bonnets. Some of the girls got new dresses from relatives; the rest of us got to pick something right off the rack—the Wardrobe rack. I always managed to find something blue. The Nazareth Guild, a Green Bay-based women's service organization, supplied Easter bonnets.

On Easter Sunday, and other holidays, the Sisters collected any gifts of candy the children received from their families and put them in a cupboard. They expected the kids to share their bounty with those who weren't as fortunate.

Christmas was, and is, my favorite time of year. December 1942, brought many delightful surprises for me because, looking back, I don't remember celebrating Christmas at home.

About two weeks before the holiday, Christmas trees started showing up in the playrooms, covered with colored lights and glass balls. The ornaments sparkled with reflections from the lights.

On the stage in the first floor auditorium, a crèche with a stable and life-sized figures depicting Jesus's birth brought the Nativity scene to life. Surrounding the stable were more evergreens decorated with blue lights and strands of silvery tinsel.

In the classrooms, the teachers told and retold the Christmas story. The students learned Christmas carols and gathered in the auditorium to practice them.

Everyone seemed to grow happier as Christmas day drew near. To my astonishment, Sister Edythe was less grumpy. She even overlooked one or two of my infractions.

On Christmas Eve, we went to bed at 6:00 p.m. and were wakened at 11:30 to get dressed for Midnight Mass.

Entering the chapel, I was awestruck. Six tall, lighted candles decorated the altar. Behind the altar were lighted trees filling the chapel with a *million* stars. Up in the choir loft Sister Muriel played the organ and everyone sang the High Mass and the songs we had practiced.

In spite of myself, I loved the inner peace I experienced whenever I entered the Chapel, but especially on Christmas Eve. Surely, the angels were here.

When the Mass ended and the music stopped, I didn't want to leave. Reluctantly, I got behind other girls for our return to bed. However, instead of leading us upstairs to our dorms, Sister Edythe took the stairs down to the playroom. Sister Rose was already there; we hadn't noticed her slipping out of chapel. As we entered the playroom, Sister Rose handed each of us a small packet of simply wrapped packages.

Emma grabbed my hand, and we ran to our favorite corner of the playroom. We jumped up and down, hugging and squealing with joy. We ripped the wrappings from our presents. Inside, we both found coloring books, crayons, and sets of jacks. I also got cutouts of movie star Betty Grable, and Emma, a scrapbook.

When the bell rang a half hour later heralding bedtime, I didn't mind. My new treasures and my friend would be there in the morning.

We awoke on Christmas morning to a breakfast of orange juice, oatmeal, toast, and milk, and on each plate, a star-shaped cookie stamped with an angel.

The Nazareth Guild ladies, and other volunteers, helped make many happy Christmases at the orphanage. They provided us with knitted slippers and pajamas. Old-fashioned hard candy was another holiday favorite supplied by the Guild. The eighth-grade girls assisted the nuns in making and sending homemade Christmas cards to prospective donors. In turn, the girls hosted an annual dinner for the group.

Regardless of how St. Joe's observed Christmas in later years, none would compare with the joy the one in 1942 brought me.

CHAPTER TWELVE

1944
The Orphanage
Angels All

My First Communion day in the spring of 1944 was a day I eagerly anticipated. I was eight years old, and what little girl does not love dressing up like a bride? I had to keep reminding myself that the important thing was not the clothes—which we were allowed to wear all day—or the festivities following the ceremony, but that I would be receiving Jesus in the Eucharist (Holy Communion).

What I had not reckoned on was what preceded the celebration—First Confession. In preparation to receive that sacrament, we had to do an examination of conscience using the Ten Commandments as a guide. Father John had been pounding the Commandments into our heads all year. Confession, Father explained, was necessary because we had to be free of sin to receive Jesus in Communion. The sacrament filled our souls with special gifts from God called graces.

As far as I was concerned, they were just another set of rules, more "musts" and "must nots," even stricter than orphanage rules. God was watching; if I messed up, he'd catch me and possibly send me to a fiery hell. If he didn't catch me, Sister Edythe would. Either way, I couldn't win.

And another thing, I had to tell my sins to a priest. I liked that requirement the least of all. I didn't believe in sharing my innermost secrets with anyone—except maybe Emma—if I didn't want. Sure, there was the "seal of confession." That meant the priest couldn't tell what I said, but could he be trusted? What if he let something slip when he was talking to someone? What if my confession was overheard by other kids? I didn't want them spreading my sins around and making me the butt of their jokes. Worst of all, what if Sister Edythe found out?

Father John instructed us that our first words would be, "Bless me, Father, for I have sinned. This is my first confession." Then we should list each sin and the number of times we committed it. After the priest gave us our penances, we'd recite the Act of Contrition.

"You must tell God you are sincerely sorry for your sins," he concluded.

Sincerity was another concept I had trouble with. How did I know if I was sincere enough? Did God have some kind of gauge by which he measured sincerity? I gritted my teeth and went about preparing myself for the ritual.

A few days before confession, I retreated to the school library with some notepaper and a pencil to sort out my sins and decide which to divulge.

Tearing through the first three commandments, I didn't see anything there to confess. I believed there was only one God. I know I loved him and would never say bad things about him. As far as keeping the Sabbath holy, there was always a nun around to make sure we did.

The fourth commandment said to "honor thy mother and thy father." I didn't have a mother or a father. Was I supposed to honor Sister Edythe? If I listed all the times I "dishonored" her, I'd be in the confessional all day.

I had to admit that I went out of my way to provoke Sister Edythe. I ignored the nun's rules, daring the woman to punish me. I talked after lights out and sassed Sister, most of the time under my breath.

There was that day the nun was on a rant. Nothing or nobody could please her. Then I did something, I don't remember what, that sent Sister Edythe over the edge. She grabbed me by the arm, dragged me over to Bosco Hall, and propelled me up the ramps to the third floor. She ordered me into a large room, empty except for a few metal beds leaning against a wall. The room ended in an empty, dark closet, which the nun shoved me into and locked the door behind me.

I tried to open the door, but it didn't budge. I dropped to the floor and curled into a ball. Blackness roiled around me, and claustrophobia set in. I closed my eyes tightly and tried to think happy thoughts, about baby kittens climbing up my arms, ponies running in grassy pastures, Joan hugging me and brushing my hair.

I don't know how long I lay in the closet before I heard the door click open. I averted my eyes until they adjusted to the light to see Sister Edythe staring down at me. She told me I was free to go. She didn't say anything else. I meekly followed her out of the room while muttering under my breath "Dear Jesus," I pleaded, "help me to not be so sassy. Help me to talk softer when I'm around Sister Edythe."

On to commandment number five. I could skip that one because I knew I never killed anyone. I don't remember what Father said about number six. I didn't know what committing adultery was so I could skip that one as well.

The seventh commandment forbade stealing. I wondered about the donut caper. Periodically the orphanage kitchen received big tins of day-old donuts from grocery stores and bakeries in Green Bay. These rare treats (not to be confused with the man-made delicacy, sauerkraut, offered up cold, and sour—which I never bothered to steal) were served in the dining room as after-school snacks. If I was on kitchen duty when the tins arrived, I gave extras to my friends and saved the gooiest for myself. Was that stealing? I wasn't sure, but I thought I'd better own up to it.

Number eight was going to be tricky: "Thou shalt not bear false witness . . ." I had said a lot of mean things about other kids, most of which were true. And I only said those things in reply to what they said to me. I hoped they were confessing their sins against me.

What about the lie Sister Nathan said I told? I hadn't, but nuns are never wrong. The way it happened was I was setting tables in the dining room when I saw Sister Nathan walking toward me. I thought it odd when she said, "Did you tell Gene that I said he couldn't leave until seven o'clock?" I nodded yes. "Well, you lied," she said. "I didn't tell him that." I suddenly realized I had misunderstood what *she* had just said. "Oh, I thought you said, '*Will* you tell Gene . . .'" She didn't let me finish. She pointed her finger at me and said, "Lying is a sin, you know."

The last two commandments had to do with "coveting." If I interpreted that correctly to mean jealousy, then I was guilty. I was jealous of girls who were prettier and more popular than me, jealous that they got all the best boyfriends, jealous when they got visitors and presents and I didn't, jealous when they got to go home. In other words, jealous of everything they had and I didn't. That was going to be a big number.

The day of my first confession, I rattled off the transgressions that were on my list. The priest asked me if I always had trouble following rules. From inside the confessional, I peered at his shadow through the dark screen and nodded. Whether or not he saw the nod, he gave me absolution.

To my surprise, I felt at peace when I left the chapel that day.

Catholics, including new communicants, couldn't eat or drink anything after midnight. (After the Second Vatican Council, between 1962 and 1965, the basic restriction changed to a one-hour fast before communion.) In the morning, I refused to brush my teeth for fear that I'd swallow some water.

At last, it was time to get dressed. The younger girls—and the older ones, too—watched in envy while we third graders donned our finery. We pulled our long, white stockings up tight, rolling the garters around the top, and buckled our white patent leather shoes. We brought our dresses carefully over our heads, so as not to mess up our hair. Sister Rose and Sister Edythe helped us affix our veils with straight pins.

We walked down the aisle with our hands folded in front of us. I thought the boys looked elegant in their dark pants, white shirts, and black ties.

Each of us received a prayer book and rosary in commemoration of our First Communion day. The Mass was said and sung in Latin with the priest facing the altar. The prayer books were written in English and Latin, making it easy to translate some of the English words to Latin.

A white, carved wooden rail separated the sanctuary from the pews. Before Communion, two altar boys drew a linen cloth over the top of the railing. We knelt at the railing, placed our hands under the cloth, and the priest placed a thin, white wafer on each of our tongues. We had been taught that touching the Host was a sin since it represented Christ's body. Nor were we supposed to chew it. We had to swallow it whole.

As we returned to our pews, I'm sure the nuns could see the halos around our heads. I put my face in my hands. For a few minutes, I was alone with my Savior. I was sure I had met him that day.

CHAPTER THIRTEEN

1945
The Orphanage
And the Angels Sing

From the first time I heard the sisters singing in church, I knew I had to be part of such a group—without becoming a nun. I longed to be part of a choir because then I could sing to my heart's content, in glorious anonymity. And to sing in the chapel's choir loft! That was tantamount to being in Heaven surrounded by angels.

When I was in fourth grade, I responded eagerly when Sister Muriel, the music teacher, announced she was holding tryouts for a children's choir. Up to that point, the sisters had made up the only choir.

The auditions were held the next day after school in the music room. A number of kids, including my friend Penny and me, signed up for the audition. When it was my turn, Sister Muriel played the scales on the piano, and my confidence grew as I carried each note. After the tryouts, I was one of about fifteen children who qualified. We had to report to the chapel at 9:00 a.m. on Saturdays.

There was nowhere on earth I would rather have been on Saturday mornings than in the chapel singing. I studied until I knew each song by heart, whether in English or Latin.

The choir sang every weekday at the early Mass for the nuns and a later Mass for the children. Once we got to sing for a Green Bay radio station.

During these moments I often thought about my sister, wondered what had happened to her, what the two of us might be doing. In time, I stopped crying every night for Joan. I was sure if my sister was alive, she would have tried to contact me.

CHAPTER FOURTEEN

The 1940s
The Orphanage
Fun and Games

Regardless of the season, I preferred being outdoors. I'd have run straight there after finishing in the classroom, but orphanage rules required that we change into play clothes first. St. Joe's was strict about which clothes were worn for what activity. The nicest dresses were reserved for Sundays, skirts and blouses for school, and older, worn-out dresses for play.

Once changed, I headed for the playground on the main building's north side. In the center of the large area was a long slide, and wooden swings that hung from heavy ropes. The girls competed on the swings to see who could pump the highest and catch a glimpse of the Fox River.

A three-foot concrete wall kept the play area separate from the ravines and farmlands beyond. That wall was an outlet for my fantasies. If I was a pirate, the wall was the plank my enemies walked. Or the wall served as my tightrope, and I was the star of the circus. Some of the girls mimicked the heroine in the movie *The Last of the Mohicans* by pretending they were jumping off a mountain. The wall was often a place to hide behind, other times a place to lean against and read, or just bask in a sun-filled day observing other kids.

Playing marbles was popular, and many beautifully colored cat-eyes changed hands on those grounds. We played "keepsies," and my cache dwindled every time I thought I could outshoot the boys.

Roller skating was popular among the girls. The metal skates came with a two-ended key. One end allowed the skates to be made smaller or larger; the other to clamp the skates to our shoes. The sidewalks between the main orphanage building and Melania, and the main building and Nazareth Hall, were the skaters' domain. The sounds of their rolling wheels echoed in the tunnels that ran beneath the sidewalks that connected the three buildings.

For skaters wanting a challenge, there was the steep sidewalk between Nazareth Hall and the bishop's house on South Webster Avenue. Try as I might, I could not get my feet to go in the same direction as the skates. I took more spills than I cared to count.

Hopscotch was another favorite outdoor activity for the girls. Sister Rose handed us chalk as we banged out the playroom door to the playground where we'd redraw the squares that the rain hadn't washed away, or create new ones.

There were structured activities year round for boys including baseball and basketball teams, which were part of Green Bay city leagues. There was also a Boy Scout troop. Girls were left to make their own entertainment.

In winter, an area on the playground was set aside and flooded for ice skating. When the weather was cold enough, some of us snuck across the road to skate on the frozen Fox River. I tried that only once. Because I had weak ankles that refused to hold me up for more than five minutes, I was less successful at ice skating than I had been at roller skating.

Looking toward the Fox River, Late 1950s
Courtesy of the Neville Public Museum of Brown County

Slopes surrounding the orphanage offered tobogganing and sledding in winter with the best sledding occurring after a fresh snowfall.

The sport had two unwritten rules: one, each child waited his or her turn; two, only four riders to a toboggan. These were immediately broken. The toboggan no sooner touched the hill's top when there was a scramble for seats. The quickest were the lucky ones, with the front usually seized by a large boy. As navigator, he had all the power and could steer the craft wherever he chose, delighting the stouthearted and terrorizing the not-so-stouthearted.

The rider on the tail end would push the toboggan off, and as many kids as could squeeze in before the craft launched filled the spaces in between. Anyone who fell—or was pushed off—was forced to trudge back up to the top and wait for the next ride down.

For me, tobogganing and other snow games, like making angels or joining in on snowball fights, will always be among my happy remembrances of St. Joe's.

The person to beat at any game in any season indoors or out was Sister Rose, who was in charge of the older girls and supervised the girls' playroom. She would play whatever she was asked. She taught us to make string figures—stars, birds, cups, and saucers—in the game of "cat's cradle." She was also good at jumping rope.

The game at which she excelled and was seldom defeated was carroms. My competitive side was determined to break her winning streak.

Popular in the 1940s, carroms was played on a wooden board with net pockets, similar to billiards pockets, in each corner. The game pieces were black-and-white, doughnut-shaped pieces known as "men." A single red one was called the "queen." The queen was placed in the board's center and surrounded by the men.

Two or four players sit opposite each other. To win each side had to pocket all its colors plus the queen. Shots were made with other game pieces called "strikers."

Those rules, like those for tobogganing, were soon forgotten. The game became another free-for-all with players slamming and banging their pieces around the board. Onlookers cheered them on, their enthusiasm expressed in jumps and shouts. The game I had seen Sister Rose and some girls playing my first night in the orphanage had been a carroms game.

After practicing shooting and pocketing for weeks, I challenged Sister Rose to a game. There were just the two of us. I went first, flicking my striker with my index finger and pocketing three or four carroms before a miss with the next piece.

Sister Rose took over with her blacks and landed several. Soon, only the queen, two blacks, and one white were left. The nun flicked in one black, then the other but missed with the queen. She had to return one black to the board.

I pocketed my last white and aimed for the queen. It slid off the board's left edge into the netting. I was the winner.

Years later, I gave one of my grandsons a carroms game for Christmas, but for him, it couldn't match the excitement of video games.

CHAPTER FIFTEEN

1946
The Orphanage
Puppy Love

"Will I ever have a boyfriend?" That's the question I pondered every time I examined my face in a bathroom mirror. I was nearly eleven and beginning to discover boys.

What boy is ever going to look at me? I'm the homeliest girl in my class. My nose was too big, and my hair too stringy. It had grown out after Sister Edythe chopped it off upon my arrival at the orphanage, and with regular haircuts (from local barbers who were brought in to do the job), I kept it at shoulder length, but it hung limp. My permanent teeth had come in and simply didn't fit in my small mouth. *Ain't it funny how so much sassiness did?* My ears, well, my ears were ugly and too big. *I'll have to keep those covered.*

On the plus side were my eyes. People told me I had pretty, brown eyes (inherited, I found out, from my great-grandfather). A couple of the girls told me I would have shapely legs when I grew up, just like the movie star Betty Grable. (I didn't get that at all.) But were my eyes and the promise of good legs enough to win me a boyfriend? I didn't think so.

That is until early September in 1946. On a Saturday morning, three girls, all atwitter, rushed into the playroom and stopped by a table Emma and I were sitting at. "Have you seen the new boy?" one of them asked. "He's so-o-o-o cute. The boys say he's good at sports."

"I wonder who his girlfriend will be," a second chimed in. Then all three dashed off to share their good news with another group in the playroom.

"Probably Karen or Janet or Sarah," I grumbled to Emma. "All the boys pick them."

I got my first look at the new boy Monday morning when I walked into the classroom. He was talking to Father John, who was there for his weekly religious instruction. The boy was nearly as tall as the priest, with dark eyes and dark wavy hair. I didn't realize I was staring until he looked at me and grinned. Embarrassed, I ran to my desk and slid down as far as I could.

Father John introduced the newcomer; his name was David. David smiled broadly at all my classmates but winked at me. After that he gave me a smile every time I looked his way.

David's game was football. One day, as he passed me in the corridor, he stopped me and asked if I had ever seen a football game. He threw some football terms at me.

When I responded with a blank stare, he said, "You know what, there's a book you oughta read. It's about Knute Rockne, a famous football player."

Okay. He's just making fun of me.

After that, I only watched David on the sly, wherever he was. Because his desk was one row over and four seats behind me in class, I had to wait until he was called on to read in order to stare at him.

One morning, before the teacher arrived, when I turned to the back of the room, hoping to have a chance to ogle surreptitiously the beautiful David, he was frowning at me.

"Now what did I do?" I mouthed at him.

He tore a page from his tablet, scribbled a few words on it, and had the note passed up to me. I opened the note and read it. "When I first came here, I liked you but you didn't like me, so now I don't like you either. I like Sarah."

I had to read the note twice before I understood it. David, the most popular boy in school, had chosen me for his girlfriend, and I was too stupid to see that.

In the end, it didn't matter that I was no longer his girlfriend. Despite my belief that I was the ugliest girl around, a boy had liked me. I shrugged, refolded the note, and stuck it in a book. I would not soon forget David.

Later that day I checked the Knute Rockne book out of the library—and read it.

CHAPTER SIXTEEN

1947
The Orphanage
Without Consent

Emma and I remained friends throughout our stay at the orphanage, and after we left. We lost track of each other for a while but renewed our friendship when my second foster home was in the same city as hers. I was a baptismal sponsor for one of her sons.

At the orphanage we shared everything the law allowed, which wasn't much other than our toys and time. Even though we were both the same size, we couldn't share clothes, courtesy of the letter-number tags sewn into every piece of clothing we wore (mine was B4). And we were certain that even if we tried to switch, Sister Edythe would know. We didn't share boyfriends; I rarely had one to share. But that didn't stop us from sharing everything we knew about boys. That wasn't going to fill up a novel anytime soon.

For a short time, our twosome became a threesome with the arrival of Penny. I liked Penny the minute I saw her. She was everything I wasn't: cute as could be with curly hair and a little button nose. Everybody liked her. She was sweet and friendly, didn't put on airs. However, she stayed only a few months at St. Joe's.

Such short stays were one of the reasons I thought I had difficulty forming lasting friendships. I'd find someone I liked, make friends with them, and then they were gone. I wasn't as approachable as some of the other kids were, in part due to my shyness. I didn't feel shy in school; my studies and hard work gave me the confidence I needed there. Outside the classroom, I felt vulnerable and alone. I didn't know how to make friends.

I would love to have been friends with Karen, the most popular girl in our sixth grade class. She was tall and beautiful and fun to be with. Everybody wanted to be around her. I watched from the sidelines while boys and girls alike fawned over her.

Four other girls whom I also considered the most popular were in my sixth grade class. Deborah, tall, smart, a leader; Mary with a sparkling personality and the voice of an angel; Sarah with lovely green eyes, flawless complexion, and witty stories about her Irish family; and cute little Janet with a figure that attracted all the boys.

While I longed to be part of the girls' activities, I held back, expecting them to ask me if they thought I fit in with their group. One day when I was alone in the playroom, Deborah and a number of other girls approached me.

"We've got something to show you," said Deborah, "but you have to come upstairs."

Unsure as to whether I should trust them, I wavered for a second. However, curiosity and the chance of acceptance into their group won me over.

Giggling, the girls led me to the third floor. There were more girls there and they formed a circle around me. "Have you ever seen a girl's breast?" Deborah asked.

When I answered no, Deborah came closer to me. "Mavis's are bigger than anyone else. Do you want to see?"

Before I could reply, Mavis, a girl I didn't know very well, opened and quickly closed her blouse. I know I blushed; I could feel the heat in my face. *Is this what they do?*

"There's something else you gotta see," Deborah spoke again as the rest of the girls departed.

When I asked where the other girls were going, Deborah replied, "They've already seen it."

She led me into the large dorm. Then checking to see that no one followed, she opened a small door in the middle of the room. She ducked down to enter and signaled me to follow her.

We were in an attic with A-shaped beams and rugged, unfinished walls. Deborah closed the door, leaving it open only to let in a sliver of light. "This is our secret," she cautioned me. "You can't tell anyone."

She knelt and told me to lie down. She lifted my dress, slid her hand down my underpants, and began to massage between my thighs. I felt my face growing hot again, but didn't move. Deborah stopped her massaging, got up, and left.

Center attic, July, 1978
Courtesy of the Diocese of Green Bay Archives

I stayed still in the semi-darkness. I was dazed and irked that someone had again thus been able to take advantage of me.

I thought back to the time when I first arrived at the orphanage. Laura, three or four years older than me, was part of a group of girls that was given charge of new arrivals. She was the same girl who changed my bed after the bedwetting incident.

After supper one day, shortly after my arrival, Laura told me that Sister Edythe had assigned her to give me a shower. There was no reason not to believe her. She took me—I was seven at the time—upstairs to the small bathroom and she sat on a closed toilet. She undressed me, set me sideways on her lap, and bent me backward until my head almost touched the floor. She slapped my crotch repeatedly.

"Do you know why I'm doing this?" Laura asked.

"No," I answered.

Laura ordered me to say, "No, Laura." I did as she requested.

"To make you a good girl," Laura said. Then she lifted me up, pushed me aside, and left.

I was bewildered now the same as I had been then. I crept out of the attic and left the third floor and dorm room. *What did the girls mean by being so hurtful?* I wanted no one to see me. I was too ashamed to tell anyone, even Emma.

CHAPTER SEVENTEEN

1946
The Orphanage
A New Era

The world and the orphanage changed in 1946. World War II was over, and many soldiers who had spent time at the orphanage came back for a visit to St. Joe's. For some of them, it was the only home they had known. Handsome in their uniforms, they turned the girls' heads, I among them.

One soldier chose to be married at St. Joe's. Mary, with her angelic voice, sang at the nuptial Mass. Later she reported being awed by the couple; he, proud in his khakis, his bride in an off-white suit.

Sister Lenore arrived to replace Sister Agatha as Sister Superior. Among the changes she introduced were school uniforms for the girls. These consisted of black A-line skirts and short-sleeved pastel blouses. The skirts had tabs at the waists that matched up with buttons on the blouses, keeping everything neatly and modestly in place. Some girls preferred the freedom of untucked blouses until a nun caught them and made them button up. When Sister turned her back, the blouses came out again.

Under Sister Lenore, the auditorium, which could accommodate up to three hundred people, got more use. Charitable organizations hosted carnival events with clowns, games, and prizes. A children's theater group put on a "Variety of Talent" benefit. The youngsters sang and danced in costumes of silk and organdy.

Some of us sixth and seventh graders—fourteen in all—put on a show of our own. Sister Lenore had taught us variations on square dances.

Sunday night movies improved. What had been mostly Westerns now included drama and musicals. While boys and girls had separate dorms and playrooms, commingling in the auditorium on movie night made it possible, with a bit of shuffling, to sit by one's beau of the week (for those lucky enough to have a beau of the week). After the lights dimmed, the furtive handholding began. Vincent—another short-term tenant—had a crush on me and made a dash for the chair next to mine. However, I only had eyes for Rick, who didn't know I was alive. Kids on punishment still went to the movies, but they had to sit in the back of the auditorium facing the wall under the watchful eyes of a nun.

First floor auditorium, July, 1978
Courtesy of the Diocese of Green Bay Archives

Another of the new Sister Superior's innovations was to get volunteers to drive us to town to see movies at the Bay Theater on Washington Street. It is now the Meyer Theater.

In the summer of 1946, we were treated to a day at Bay Beach. Located along the bay of Green Bay, Bay Beach was a favorite recreation spot, with a pavilion where, during the 1940s, you could dance, or roller skate, for fifteen cents. You danced to such big names as Glen Miller and Tommy Dorsey. Lawrence Welk drew a crowd of more than one thousand people when he came in 1944. In 1935, President Franklin Delano Roosevelt visited Bay Beach; thousands came to hear him speak.

In those days, you could still swim in the bay, before it became too polluted. Today Bay Beach is a great place for a family outing with inexpensive rides, picnic and play areas, pony rides, a small-scale Wisconsin Central passenger train ride. And as of 2011, the Zippin Pippin roller coaster.

Sister Lenore arranged for us to be transported to Bay Beach, standing up in pickup trucks. I spent the day swimming, missed out on the roller skating. I don't remember what we ate. What I do remember best about that outing is the most delicious drink I had ever tasted. Pepsi-Cola. How do I know it was Pepsi? A small plane flying above the park pulled a banner that attested to the fact.

In late summers, during the blueberry season, some of the kids—three or four at a time—were chosen to accompany one of the nuns and Father John to a priest's cottage in northern Michigan. I won that lottery in 1948. Good behavior was the price of a ticket. Imagine that. I must have gotten away with something. Or maybe I was finally wising up . . . Nah.

The day brought both joy and sadness for me. I remember blue skies, warm sunshine, and the fresh open air. We spent the day swimming, boating, picnicking, and picking blueberries. We even got to eat some of them. For a little while, I forgot where I lived, but I also missed the family that I had lost. What would we be doing on a day like this?

One of the changes Sister Lenore introduced, and which all of us dreaded, was spankings with the black rubber hose she kept in her office.

I've never forgotten my singular encounter with that black tube. I was ten at the time. I had disregarded the no-talking-after-lights-out bell once too often, and was written up and put on the punishment roster, earning myself a trip to Sister Lenore's office.

The trek to Sister's office, as reported by those in the know, was nothing as grand as a march with another sister dragging us by the ear. No, we had to go by ourselves and stand outside Sister Lenore's office until she was ready for us. And she gave us plenty of time to think about our crimes. By the time Sister called me to come in, my defiance had taken a hike.

She opened the single door inside her office and told me to go into the windowless room. She clicked on a light, closed the door, and went to a cupboard inside the room. When she turned around, I saw she held a piece of hose about twenty-five inches long. I had heard horror stories about the thing, but had never come face-to-face with it. Sister Lenore told me to lie over the chair. I reluctantly let out a yelp the first time the hose struck my backside, then recoiled and clenched my teeth for the next blow, and the next, and the next. I vowed that I would never again get caught talking after hours.

But now I belonged to the "rubber hose" fraternity and had my own firsthand account to share with my friends.

CHAPTER EIGHTEEN

1948
The Orphanage
Sewing Bee

My lifelong love for sewing began when I was twelve and assigned as Sister Amanda's helper in the Wardrobe, the storehouse for the girls' clothing.

My job was to go through the piles of clothing that came in from outside charitable organizations, sort them by size, and set aside those that needed mending. Sister Amanda was a gentle, soft-spoken nun. She was also a whiz at fixing torn clothes and constructing new garments on her treadle sewing machine. I hounded her daily with questions about her craft.

One day when I walked into the Wardrobe, there was a bolt of pink-and-gray flowered fabric on the long table in the center of the room. Sister Amanda asked me if I'd like learn to make a dress. "Oh, yes," I replied.

Sister Amanda had selected a dress pattern that she used often. She took the pattern pieces out of the envelope and showed me how to lay them out so that no fabric was wasted. She taught me how to read the markings on the pattern. Then she left me alone to pin the pieces onto the fabric and cut them out.

During the next few weeks, Sister Amanda very patiently demonstrated the art of dressmaking, from seams to facings, to gathering and attaching sleeves, to hand-stitching buttonholes. One of the neatest things I learned from her was how to make a blind hem, taking tiny stitches that were almost invisible to the naked eye.

On my thirteenth birthday, Sister Amanda presented me with five yards of light blue fabric to do with as I wished. I didn't have to think long; I knew exactly what I'd do with it. Make a dance costume like one I'd seen in *The Red Shoes*, one of the movies shown on movie night (sometime in 1948 or '49, when I was twelve years old).

The story was about a ballerina, based on a Hans Christian Anderson fairy tale. The dancer, played by actress Moira Shearer, was torn between her desire to become a prima ballerina and the man she loved. I dreamed and dreamed of the day when I could be a dancer just like the starlet in the movie. Of course, I'd have to find a way to split my time in two, what with my intention to own and operate a horse ranch . . . *OK, horse ranch by day, dancer by night.*

Every day for three weeks, I worked on my project, sewing each piece by hand. The top was plain, sleeveless, collarless, and lined. It took four petticoats, each with a five-inch ruffle around the bottom, to make the top skirt fluff out the way it was meant to. I finished the costume with hand-stitched buttonholes and white pearl buttons.

Pleased with the finished product, I modeled it for Sister Amanda, who lavishly praised my fashion debut.

I wore the costume and danced every chance I got, but only in the dorm and when Sister Edythe wasn't around. And because I was sure she would not approve of anything as frivolous as a dance costume, kept it hidden in my nightstand.

One evening when I went to get the costume, it wasn't there. None of the girls in my dorm had seen it. After searching in the Wardrobe, I was returning to my room, tears in my eyes, when I saw Sister Edythe. The words uttered by her didn't matter to me—something about evil and the devil's work. The triumphant look in the nun's eyes did; she had found a way to punish me. I felt crushed and angry and helpless.

I never did find out how Sister Edythe discovered my costume, but that did not alter the way I felt for having created it.

CHAPTER NINETEEN

1948
The Orphanage
Growing Up

Two major events/milestones happened in 1948 when I was twelve years old and in the seventh grade. That was the year I won the first "Spelldown" and the year I got my period.

Sister Lenore introduced the spelldowns, competitions much like today's spelling bees. Children who wanted to participate got lists of words from their teachers and then had two weeks to study. We studied in pairs or small groups, testing each other on the words.

On the day of the Spelldown, children, teachers, and supervisors took their seats in the auditorium. Contestants sat in the front rows. Sister Lenore gave us each a word to spell in turn. As long as we spelled it correctly, we remained standing.

One by one, the contestants were eliminated until I was the last one standing. "Congratulations" was my final word to spell.

As I left the stage, I heard a familiar voice behind me. "Congratulations," it said, echoing the winning word. The voice was Sister Edythe's; for once, it was without malice. So was her smile.

"You deserved to win," she said. "I never saw anyone study so hard."

Astonished by her unexpected kindness, I swallowed and whispered my thanks. A few minutes later, I heard Sister Edythe berating some of my classmates standing by.

"If you had studied as much as Beatrice did, you could have been winners too," she told them. "Next time more study and less play."

"Yes, 'stir," the kids answered.

"That's 'yes, Sister.'" The malice was back in her voice. "Did you hear me? You say, 'Yes, Sister.' Now let me hear that said correctly."

"Yes, *Sister,*" they chorused. I could see the smirk on Sister Edythe's face as she turned and walked away.

I watched my classmates. When they were sure Sister was no longer watching, one boy made a rude gesture in her direction. Two girls thumbed their noses at her. I put my head down and smiled. Sometimes I wondered if the nun knew or even cared what the orphans thought of her.

As the winner, I received the grand prize of two dollars and a chaperoned trip to downtown Green Bay to spend it. I bought a Kodak Brownie camera and two rolls of film.

Around the same time that year, I got my period for the first time. Until then, I didn't know what a "period," or the "monthly," was. That's what the girls called it; they said it involved bleeding. One girl knowingly warned that anyone missing her "monthly" was going to have a baby.

Then one day it happened to me. The day I found blood in my underpants, I was so embarrassed that the only person I told was Emma. She said I'd have to tell Sister Edythe in order to get the "stuff" I needed. She added that she hadn't gotten her period yet.

Having to tell that nun something this personal galled the heck out of me. I waited until Sister was alone before approaching her. The nun told me to return to my dorm while she got the necessary supplies.

I had intended to keep the whole episode private. Imagine my chagrin when Sister Edythe returned to the dorm room where a number of girls had gathered, with this paraphernalia dangling from her hands. I put my head down and followed her out of the room.

In the bathroom, I felt humiliated as Sister Edythe fastened the garter-like contraption with its accompanying gauze pad to my bare bottom. Back in the dorm, Sarah whispered to me that she had gotten her period that day too. I could have hugged her for trying to cheer me up. I hated the thought of being stuck with this stupid thing for the rest of my life. Most of the other girls did not seem to mind. To them it meant they were now a woman.

Do the boys know about this? I pondered the question. *Wouldn't that be awful if they did!*

The Sisters kept any conversation about "monthlies" quiet around boys, but I'm sure some of the girls *talked.* If a boy got too curious about the subject, any nun overhearing assigned extra arithmetic problems as punishment. Some boys were becoming quite proficient at multiplication and long division.

CHAPTER TWENTY

1949 – 1950
The Orphanage
Queen for a Day

My hard work in school finally paid off in the spring of 1949 when Sister Lenore chose me as May Queen for the orphanage's May Day celebration.

The celebration took place on the lawn in front of St. Joe's. The children formed a living rosary. The girls dressed in navy blue skirts, white blouses and veils, and represented the "Hail Marys"; the boys in dark pants and white shirts represented the "Our Fathers" and the "Glory Bes." The Queen, wearing a white dress and a crown of flowers, placed a similar crown on the head of the Blessed Virgin's statue.

Just before the event, I found myself in trouble again. I was coming out of my classroom when I saw Sister Lenore coming out of her office. I tried to avoid the nun by turning the other way.

Sister Lenore saw me, however, and called to me to stop. She put her hands on my head and fluffed my hair. "Let's get you some curls," she said. Some of the other girls had gotten permanents, and she had been pleased with those.

The suggestion stunned me. If I wanted curls, I could tie rag strips in my hair the night before and be curly in the morning. It was nobody's business but mine how I fixed or wore my hair.

"No," I blurted out. "I'm not going to let anyone put that junk in my hair." I did remember some of the girls getting perms and I thought they stunk like crazy.

Sister Lenore gasped and stared at me, then slapped me hard across the face.

My May Queen honor was rescinded, given instead to a "more popular" girl, one who had had a permanent. I hid my resentment while scolding myself: *When will you learn to keep your big mouth shut?*

Eighth grade in 1950 brought the Sacrament of Confirmation, and graduation. Prior to the events, our confirmation sponsors took us shopping for clothes. The ladies of the Nazareth Guild paid for our dresses and shoes, and for the corsages we wore.

Bishop Stanislaus Vincent Bona confirmed us at St. Francis Xavier Cathedral in Green Bay. I chose the name of Rose for my confirmation name.

A week later, after the graduation Mass, nine graduates, five girls and four boys, had their picture taken with the bishop on the back steps of the bishop's home.

For me, graduation was like release from prison. It meant no more bells ordering my day, no more strict rules governing my conduct and, best of all, no more Sister Edythe spying on me. I was sure that once I left the orphanage, I could do exactly as I pleased.

Years later when some of us *orphans* held informal reunions, we agreed that our years at the orphanage had been a mixed bag. On the one hand, we realized we might have been better off at the orphanage than in homes where parents were absent, drunk, or child abusers. On the other, while at St. Joe's, we never knew a parent's love and we never got the individual attention we needed. "Love, never; discipline, ever" was a theme developed by our experiences.

The nuns had not prepared us for the real world. We didn't know how to handle money or how to get a job. Our cultural experiences were limited to watching movies and playing games. While *please* and *thank you* had been drummed into our stubborn little heads, we had been taught no other social skills. We had been given no advice for real living, for real life. Who teaches a child how to love?

I believe crimes of apathy and indifference take second billing only to abuse, whether committed behind the doors of an institution or the doors of a dysfunctional home.

At one reunion while we reminisced about our dislike for Sister Edythe, we also wondered what happened to her.

"Oh, she became Sister Superior later on," said one of the men. "Everyone liked her."

"Everyone liked her?" someone asked with raised eyebrows. The speaker nodded. Who would have guessed?

We came together with similar childhood stories and it helped put our lives in perspective. We waded through our feelings of uncertainty, inadequacy, insecurity, and inferiority. We were ashamed that we had been raised in an orphanage. We thought it was our fault that nobody wanted us, that there was something wrong with us. We had no idea what the world was all about, so after we were "released", for us, it was a game of survival. I believe our experiences made us who we are, good or bad. It also made us strong.

CHAPTER TWENTY ONE

1950 – 1952
Northern Wisconsin
Deliverance

U pon completing eighth grade, those children still residing at St. Joseph's Orphanage with no family member willing or able to take them in, were placed in foster homes where they remained until the age of eighteen. The Apostolate made those arrangements. There were nine of us diehards in my eighth grade graduating class. We received certificates of entrance to high school. Anyone not making passing grades received certificates of discharge which did not permit their entrance into high school.

About two weeks before graduation, Sister Lenore called me into her office and told me that a couple from a community north of Green Bay was considering being my foster parents. A week later they came to meet me. The man didn't say much, although he kept a steady smile on his face. The woman carried on a conversation with Sister while we walked around the grounds. My only thought was that here were my saviors; they were getting me out of this place. I was thrilled I'd finally be leaving the orphanage. What would life be like with foster parents? Would all my dreams come true? A frilly bedroom decorated in blue, new clothes, and lots of friends?

Driving away from the orphanage the day the couple came to get me, I turned for one last look at the *castle*, and the window where I had spent hours dreaming of this day. An unbidden melancholy came over me. My existence for the last eight years, while not one I had aspired to, had sheltered me from the outside world. I needed to find a way to disentangle myself from that security blanket. I resolved not to tell anyone where I had been or what had happened to me; I would bury those demons very deep and never look back.

Main entrance, 1978
Courtesy of the Diocese of Green Bay Archives

St. Joseph Orphanage, front view, 1960s
Courtesy of the Diocese of Green Bay Archives

My foster family lived in a two-story house on Main Street in a small town where everything was close by. Riding through town that first day felt like being on a movie set where all the buildings were just fronts, everyone was an actor, and at the end of the day they went back to their homes and reality. I had no end of day reality; this was a new beginning for me. I would have to create my own brand new reality. What would it be like, and where would it take me? Only I could determine that.

I did get my own bedroom, though not the frilly one I had dreamed about. One of the things I especially liked was having three rambunctious young boys, three, five, and eight, to look after. They reminded me of the brothers I might have grown up with.

But to say that I felt like I belonged would be less than accurate. While I never felt like a servant, neither did I feel like a member of the family. Normal family living, children interacting with their parents, had no reality for me. My expectation was that I was there to work, and that fact was never argued.

The chores did not present a problem for me whether babysitting, cleaning, or ironing. But giving me free rein in the kitchen was probably not a good idea. I had learned to peel potatoes and frost hot cross buns at St. Joe's but nothing about planning and preparing meals. So whenever I was the cook *du jour*, I served my specialty, a concoction resembling meatloaf hamburgers. After suffering through weeks of this thoroughly tiresome fare, the ever-patient man of the house, with me in full hearing, asked his wife, "Could we have something different once in a while?"

My problem once again was making friends in my new environment. As usual, my shyness got in the way. The kids I met had grown up in families with two parents—a fact that surprised me. Every kid I had known up to this point in my life had come from a broken home. These kids all had childhood friends whom they had gone to school with from kindergarten on. Most had nice clothes. I wore orphanage hand-me-downs. I was the stranger in town, alone. I had no one and belonged to no one.

One morning, not long after my placement in the foster home, while trying to deal with these feelings of inferiority, the front doorbell rang. When I answered it, to my amazement, Janet was standing there. After gaping for a moment or two, I said, "Hi, what are you doing here?"

"Hi," she returned my greeting and proceeded to fill me in.

"Right after you left, I found out I was going to a family in the same town as you. The two ladies know each other. The house is over on State Street, not too far from here. C'mon, I'll show you."

Without thinking—and stupidly, I'll have to admit—I followed Janet without telling anyone where I was going. When I returned, about an hour later, my foster mother read me the riot act, but good. She told me I was not allowed to go anywhere without asking her permission first.

Though Janet and I had not been close friends at the orphanage, I was delighted to now have someone with whom I could relate.

Over the summer we became best friends and spent most of our free time together, either at the movies (television had not yet made its way to this part of Wisconsin) or the town's teen hot spot, the corner soda fountain, drinking cherry cokes and dropping nickels in the juke box. Listening to the likes of Nat King Cole, The Ames Brothers, Theresa Brewer, and Patti Page. The establishment had just enough room for dancing, and before long we joined the fun, learning to do the jitterbug, even changing partners with some of the other girls. The boys who weren't "taken" stood safely on the sidelines watching, sizing up the remaining eligibles.

The fact that Janet attracted most of the boys in the room never seemed to translate into fallout dates for me—on the contrary, in fact. Even when Sadie Hawkins day came around (Leap Year day, when girls get to ask boys for a date). I asked one boy, but he turned me down flat, enhancing my notion that snagging a boyfriend could be a life-long battle for me.

But snag one I did. I met him at the movies. I was with Janet, and he stopped by our row, leaned in and asked, "This seat taken?" indicating the seat next to mine. Surprised, I turned to Janet and shrugged. She poked me in the ribs—hard—and whispered, "Tell him no, it isn't." I glanced up at him and shook my head. With a big grin on his face, he plunked himself down.

"Hi, my name is Herman, but everyone calls me Herm."

During the movie, we took turns sneaking peaks at each other. Mine were of a curious nature. *Who is this blond boy who chose to sit next to me? And why did he choose me?* His were more of a disconcerting nature, with a permanent all-knowing grin. After the movie, I told him I had to go right home.

"Oh, really," he said.

Was that a look of disappointment?

"Yes," I answered.

"Ok . . . Well, I'll see you around."

"What'd you think?" I asked Janet as soon as he was out of earshot.

"I think he's cute, and he likes you. I think you should *go* with him." *Going* with a boy meant you were going steady.

"I don't think my foster mother would approve."

"She doesn't have to know."

Herm and I started meeting at the soda fountain. I found out he was a year younger than me, so we wouldn't be seeing each other in school that year. When I think of it now, I chuckle to myself. *What high school girl—though only a lowly freshman—would even think of going out with an eighth grader?*

We'd meet at the theater, sit in the dark eating popcorn, and he'd read the Deep Rock gas station ads up on the screen out loud.

"Hiiiiii, Deep Rock!"

We saw the likes of *It's a Wonderful World* with James Stewart, and Westerns like *She wore a Yellow Ribbon* with John Wayne. I liked the Spencer Tracy/Katharine Hepburn comedies like *Adam's Rib. I* could relate—in a way—to *Johnny Belinda* with Jane Wyman, and loved romances like *The Heiress* with Olivia DeHavilland.

Then one day it happened. Herm had gotten to the theater before me, as usual, only this time he had chosen a seat in the back row. I smiled weakly as I sat down next to him. I had observed that the last row in a darkened movie theater existed for one purpose: making out. Midway through the main feature, he shuffled in his seat. Slowly he inched his arm around the back of the seat and up toward my shoulder. That's as far as he got. I leaned forward, turned and gave him a dirty look. Coming from the strict religious environment that I had, I wasn't sure what was right and proper in the romance—or making out—department. He didn't try that again for a while. Eventually he got up the courage to give me a peck on the cheek, and not long after, one straight out on my lips. I don't remember carrying on and swooning like the ladies in the movies did . . . well, maybe a little.

As September approached, I looked forward to classes at the local high school. I thought I'd be more in my element in that setting, and it would give me a chance to meet more kids my age. Instead, it nearly turned out to be my undoing. The first day freshmen met as a class we were asked to each stand and tell which grade school we had graduated from. Besides the public elementary school, there was one Catholic grade school in the town, and I hadn't graduated from either. I shifted nervously in my desk as each student rose and named her or his alma mater.

As my turn neared, I knew I couldn't say I had gone to one of the local grade schools, the students who had gone there would know I was lying. When I blurted out "St. Joseph's Orphanage," my answer was met with stares and whispers. I wanted to crawl in a hole.

For a moment, I wished I were back in Green Bay, behind the safety of that institution's walls. At least there I fit in. I rejected my classmates' stares. If they assumed my parents were dead, I'd let them.

Once again, school proved the place where I was most comfortable. I joined the glee club and as a sophomore tried out for basketball, playing guard. My competitiveness served me well there. I was assigned to guard one of the more aggressive players, giving my rank *insecurity complex* a welcome jolt.

As soon as I turned sixteen, I signed up for drivers' education. My first road trip inspired a wild essay for my English class. Three were selected to be read in front of the class. Much to my dismay, mine was one of them.

When the teacher called my name, I put my hands in my lap and sank deep into my desk, thinking to become invisible. My throat went dry. Seeing no escape, clenching my fingers around the paper, I dragged myself to the front of the room. The words on the paper spun past as I read through the piece. My epic fantasy adventure told of roaring around winding roads on two wheels and hitting the brakes just shy of slamming into a mountain.

Never again, I vowed as I returned to my seat. I'd tone down future assignments.

My foster mother gave me a certain amount of freedom for after-school activities—which included going to the movies and the town's juke joint—as long as she didn't need me for anything. I made a few new friends, and occasionally I was allowed an overnighter at their homes where we'd spend the night reading Betty and Veronica "best friends and worst enemies" comic books, or huddled under the covers with a flashlight and the occasional movie scandal magazine. But most of the time we talked and giggled about boys.

The summer before my sophomore year, Janet told me she was going to a new foster home in Green Bay. We promised to stay in touch, and we still do to this day.

Herm and I became an "item". He had introduced me to his sister and I spent a portion of my free time hanging out at their house.

Right up until the time I left that small town.

The original rebel, I still found it difficult to follow all the rules all the time. My rebellious streak asserted itself from time to time, and on a spring evening in 1952, I found myself in serious trouble.

I had invited Herm over while I babysat, something I knew I wasn't allowed to do. He must have told his friends. The word spread and about a dozen kids showed up.

Soon the kids were getting rowdy, some of them making out in various rooms of the house. The couple came home early. I scrambled to get everyone out of the house. One kid was found hiding under the front room piano and my foster mother ordered him to leave. She sent me to my bedroom. I sat on the bed scared and dispirited. I heard her tell her husband, "She's going to end up pregnant." Even in my naiveté, I knew that was not possible. It troubled me that that was what she thought.

The next morning she called me down for a serious discussion. Stubborn and defensive, I refused to talk to her. She asked if I was unhappy, did I want to leave. In a snippy voice I answered, "I don't care."

My bravado had a sobering and unexpected result: another child welfare worker and another trip to Green Bay, this time to the Good Shepherd's Home, a facility for wayward girls operated by the Sisters of the Sorrowful Mother.

The facility was located on the corner of Porlier Street and South Webster near the hospitals (St. Vincent, St. Mary, and Bellin). It had high walls and a front gate where the worker had to ring a bell that couldn't be heard from outside, and eventually a panel opened to see who was there. Then sounds of bolts and a huge door opening to admit us. I couldn't dream stuff this scary.

The Good Shepherd's Home was actually two facilities separated by a courtyard. The Sacred Heart side housed unwed, pregnant girls; the Victorian side housed the other "bad" girls. I never met any of the pregnant teens. For my part, I minded my own business, took high school classes, and sewed in my free time, all at the Home. I became more withdrawn, angry at having been dumped in another institution. There I remained for the last three months of my sophomore year.

When the time came for me to leave, I told a girl I had befriended that I didn't want to go. "I feel safe here. I don't think I can handle life on the outside in another foster home." If I had expected to find some sort of magic in my last foster home, I had been disappointed.

But I was not the one making decisions about my life. The Apostolate had found another foster home for me.

CHAPTER TWENTY TWO

June 1952 – June 1954
Green Bay
A Family

After three months at Good Shepherd's, the Apostolate placed me in a second foster home, this time in Green Bay. And in that home is where I learned what family life was all about. Brad and Bev Jones treated me like a member of the family. Their children, three girls and a boy, ranged in ages from two to nine. Another daughter was born while I lived with the Joneses.

Brad, an attorney, had lost his right arm in a farming accident, but that didn't stop him from doing most things. He was an avid golfer and a very good swimmer. Well educated, Bev stayed home with her family and involved herself in charitable organizations.

Given the choice of attending St. Joseph Academy, an all-girls school, or Green Bay East High School, I chose the Academy because I believed it to be the more prestigious of the two schools, thereby offering a better education. I also liked that it was a Catholic institution. We wore uniforms, white blouses and navy-blue skirts, so I knew I wouldn't be judged by my clothes, at least not in the classroom. And since it was an all-girls school, there wouldn't be the distraction of boys—not that I didn't want to be distracted by boys. It's just that the boys never noticed me anyway. However, anyone driving down Monroe Avenue during the lunch hour could see Academy girls strolling up and down the sidewalk flirting with boys from Central Catholic High School cruising by in their convertibles or old tin jalopies.

Outside of school, Mrs. Jones shared her sewing machine with me, allowing me to indulge in my favorite pastime, sewing, making my own clothes, including formals for the Academy's Junior Prom and Senior Ball. The Jones girls' dolls were the best dressed in town, with everything from shorts to fancy ball gowns copied from pictures in books and magazines.

The first television station in Green Bay, WBAY-TV, signed on the air March 17, 1953. My foster father had driven to Milwaukee to purchase a television set and we all gathered around to watch the news. The final showing that evening was a movie about the life of Franz Schubert, an Austrian composer. It was my introduction to classical music and I was completely mesmerized. His *Serenade* and *Ave Maria* have stayed with me my entire life.

There was a popular television show on during the 1950s, hosted by Bishop Fulton J. Sheen, *Life is Worth Living*. At the 1952 Emmy Awards, he defeated Edward R. Murrow, Lucille Ball, and Arthur Godfrey for the title of Most Outstanding Television Personality. Even as a teenager, I was impressed with the dramatic and humorous Bishop Sheen; you just had to be.

My talent for sewing led to a television debut on WBAY-TV. One of the channel's early offerings was a popular daytime program called *A Day with Eddy Jason*—a Johnny Carson-type variety show starring Eddy Jason and Helen Day. It aired during the 1950s. Mrs. Jones's next-door neighbor knew Helen Day, and she was able to get me a spot demonstrating my doll clothes.

Appearance on WBAY-TV, Green Bay, 1954
Demonstrating my handmade doll clothes

Dressed in my uniform, I went to the studio right after school. During the on-air interview, I presented my best work, including one doll dressed as a bride. After the interview, people phoned with orders for doll clothes, but with my inherent shyness and lack of communication skills, the calls went unanswered.

The family spent summers at their cottage north of Green Bay on the bayside of Wisconsin's peninsula. Though I would have preferred to be in town and hang out with Janet, the daily swims nearly evened the score. The water was a lot cleaner back then. I learned to swim and water ski (on a single board).

Not knowing how to cook didn't stop me from trying. During my second summer at the cottage, I found a recipe for homemade root beer and decided to go for it. I found a package of root beer extract at a local grocery and, following the recipe on the back, mixed it with water, sugar, and yeast and poured it in a glass gallon jug. I screwed the cap on—the tighter, the better, I thought—and went swimming. After a while in the water, I was eager to see how my *experiment* had turned out, so I headed back up to the cottage.

The bottle was nowhere in sight. While I had been enjoying myself in the Bay, the bottle had unceremoniously blown its top. I didn't get to see the mess that must have made; Mrs. Jones had it all cleaned up before I got back, without one word of complaint. Remorse kept me out of cookbooks for a short time after that.

The root beer incident, and I'm sure there were many others, led to some teasing. My foster father wrote in my senior yearbook, "Your finishing high school indicates that you are a better student than a cook." He signed the note, "Pa." My foster mother wrote me a very nice note. All their kids signed my yearbook as well, including the baby—she had a little help.

Janet and I had been able to link up again. She was very happy with her second foster home, a family with six girls and one boy. They treated her like one of their daughters/sisters; still do.

We attended different schools. She went to East High while I went to the Academy. The two of us went to the Friday night dances at Central Catholic High, an all-boys school. There were live performances, some by well-known bands.

Every chance we got, we took the bus to Bay Beach for dances or roller skating at the pavilion. When I found out that bandleader Harry James was scheduled to appear, I bought tickets well in advance. I just had to meet the man who had won Betty Grable's heart. I remembered the hours Emma and I had spent at the orphanage playing with Betty Grable paper dolls.

In preparation for the event, I made new skirts and blouses for us. We arrived early but didn't get the close look we were hoping for. The stage was a good four feet above the dance floor. We had to settle for admiring from afar. We concluded that although James could play a mean trumpet, he wasn't as handsome as crooner Bing Crosby, Janet's favorite movie star.

Janet introduced me to one of her former boyfriends with the nickname Smiley. He was a dyed-in-the-wool country-western boy who liked singer Hank Williams. We dated for a few months. He was my date for the Junior Prom at the Academy. I stayed out too late one night, just talking and mooning over him and forgot the time. It was well past midnight by the time I got home. I had to ring the doorbell to get in, and the look on Mrs. Jones's face was all the punishment I needed.

My love affair with horses began at a very early age, probably from pictures in storybooks. I learned to appreciate their grace and beauty when I saw them running wild in a field on the way to the orphanage, and later in books and movies. These days I go weak-kneed and turn mushy inside at the sight of horses. I actually purr.

I remember one time visiting the Joneses at their cottage and watching—jealously—Mr. Jones riding horseback on the beach. I've been to the Arlington racetrack in Minnesota, not for the races, but to hang out with friends and see the wondrous creatures close up.

My first experience meeting one up close and personal was during my junior year in high school when my boyfriend Smiley invited me for an afternoon of riding with some of his friends. The bunch of us went to a horse ranch near Green Bay. The owner assured us first-time riders that the horses in the large enclosure were well trained and gentle. Smiley picked one of the smaller horses for me, and the owner brought it round. I just had to get my hands on that horse. I stroked his mane and his head while I talked to him. Smiley helped me mount before mounting his horse.

The ride took us through woody areas, grassy fields, and streams. Whenever my horse went up or down an embankment, I locked my legs around his belly and gripped the saddle horn and reins. I was fearful, and at the same time, exhilarated. When we got back and dismounted, my legs felt like rubber, but I hated to see the day end. I knew this love would last forever. I eventually broke up with Smiley, but horses own part of my heart.

My best friend at the Academy was a girl named Phoebe. Her looks and personality—two things I sadly lacked—were what attracted me to her in the first place. Tall and slim, Phoebe had dark hair, dark eyes, and a personality and smile that kept the boys panting. I met her family and spent a lot of time at her house.

During our senior year, Phoebe had to drive to Milwaukee to take her pre-entrance exams for nursing school. It was a school day. The Academy excused Phoebe, but I skipped classes to go with her. On the way home, Phoebe was speeding, she missed a curve, and the car flew into a low-lying field. Neither of us was hurt, but I had to face my foster parents with the knowledge that I had lied.

Phoebe lined up a blind date for me for the Senior Ball, I suspect from a list of her many admirers. I had already made myself a dress out of soft yellow crinoline with layers of ruffles, and had no one to go with. I reciprocated by making her prom dress.

The night of the Ball at the Hotel Northland, Phoebe introduced me to the young man, a boy of medium height with light brown hair. When the evening was over, he wrote on my dance card: THE NIGHT. THE LIGHT. THE MUSIC. THE GIRL. LOVE, WOODY.

That was the only time I ever saw him.

At the end of our senior year, we were required to attend a lecture presented by a doctor and the chaplain (the '50s version of sex education). There was a question and answer session with the doctor, and as expected, the girls presented the doctor with many questions; we won't go into them here. The chaplain's sermon ended with the following: "Remember girls, the anticipation is far greater than the realization." At the time, I didn't dwell on the bit of wisdom that was being passed on to us, and now I have no comment. My sense of humor these days sometimes needs a polish.

The two years I spent with the Joneses are among my happiest memories, though I'm sure I didn't appreciate my foster parents at the time. It took many years, after I had raised my own family, to realize that I had been part of a wonderful and special family. Brad and Bev always gave me the benefit of the doubt. I was not an easy person to know. I kept my feelings to myself while at the same time acting the part of a know-it-all. I kept in touch with the family after I left.

But in June of 1954, what was on my mind was getting on with the next phase of my life. I had worlds to conquer, after all.

CHAPTER TWENTY THREE

1954 – 1955
Green Bay
On My Own

Before graduating from high school in June of 1954, I realized in order for me to live in the real world I would need to get a job, and the job would have to start the day after graduation. It didn't occur to me to go to college. I had no money, and actually, I was glad to get away from anything institutional. But I had to earn a living, and charity was never an option.

Phoebe lined up my first job before graduation day, working in the sterilizing room at St. Vincent Hospital. Not the lofty position I had expected after graduating from St. Joseph Academy, but it would allow me to eat regularly. Phoebe had been a volunteer at the hospital during our senior year in high school. I thought she was doing me a favor, that maybe I could work my way up to something more "world-conquering."

Phoebe also helped me with my first apartment; it was owned by one of her relatives. The hospital was a mile from the apartment, and since I owned neither bicycle nor car, I walked to and from my job.

The apartment took up the back end of the first floor of an old two-story house in Green Bay near downtown. My three roommates and I shared two bedrooms, a kitchenette, and a bath, each paying seven dollars a week for the privilege. The front of the building housed the owners' insurance agency office and they lived on the second floor. One of my roommates was the insurance agency secretary.

The Bay Theater was a half mile from my apartment, serving to indulge my passion for movies. The stores, for now at least, only provided opportunities to window-shop. When I could afford a sewing machine, I planned to copy the fashions in the windows.

I did give into a whim once. Seeing a pair of ballet toe shoes in a shoe store reminded me of a favorite movie, *The Red Shoes*, and the blue costume I had sewn under Sister Amanda's guidance. I bought the shoes. Unfortunately, my weak ankles prevented my using them very often. I hid them in a drawer where they reside today.

I did not share my past with my roommates. Free for the first time in my life, I could do as I pleased, answer to no one. I tried smoking but couldn't stand the coughing after I lit up. I tried drinking beer, but it tasted bitter. Who needed it?

Men were another problem. My relationships only lasted months, or weeks, sometimes a day, more than likely due to the fact that what interested me most was dancing to whatever tune happened to be playing on the juke box, and if the chap didn't meet my expectations, I let him know it. Not a good formula for hanging on to a guy.

Nothing pleased me. Everything was a disappointment. Janet had married and moved to Mississippi with her husband. Phoebe, now in nursing school, didn't maintain contact with me. Roommates came and went. I felt my past was an albatross dragging my spirits into the ground.

I often felt that the years at the orphanage were lost years, that I was born the day I left—naïve to a fault—that I had to constantly play catch up with the rest of the world, figure everything out for myself.

In the midst of my dissatisfaction, the insurance agency secretary resigned, and I was hired in her place. The stage was now set for the next major change in my life. I was about to meet the man I would marry.

PART TWO

The magic of first love is our ignorance that it can never end.

—Benjamin Disraeli, 1804–1881

CHAPTER TWENTY FOUR

October 1955
Green Bay
First Love

I felt content for the first time in a long time that Friday morning as I sat at my desk. I had been working at the insurance agency in its two-person office as its secretary for about eight months. My office was in the front of the building, looking out on the street; it could have been a sitting room prior to being converted to office space. The big picture window beside my desk gave me a view of the outdoors, the comings and goings of cars in the street, and also of the apartment building across the street. Behind my desk was a brick fireplace. A long, high credenza with a Formica countertop and multiple drawers separated the front entryway from my office.

Working at the agency had one special benefit for me. I finally made enough money to buy my first sewing machine; I chose an inexpensive White. My wardrobe increased exponentially after that purchase.

My boss's office was adjacent to mine through a large, framed doorway. His desk was positioned so he could see into the outer office. I liked my boss, F. Charles Smith, Charlie for short. And I liked what I did—taking dictation, typing, filing. This is what I had been trained to do at St. Joseph Academy.

The day reflected my mood. A mid-October sun shone through the window that morning. A slight breeze chased leaves up the street. Those that hadn't fallen yet, a few yellow and orange, clung to nearby maple trees. I thought for a moment about Joan and my other siblings, but only for a moment. They were no longer part of my life. The protective shell I had let harden around me at the orphanage was beginning to crack.

The agency doorbell's jangling broke my reverie and got my attention. So did the young man who walked in. He was tall and movie-star handsome.

His eyes were blue and dreamy, his hair dark and wavy. I couldn't take my eyes off of him.

Charlie, upon seeing who it was, walked over to the counter and held out his hand. "How are you, Ken? How's your mother?" he asked. "How long have you been back from Korea?"

Ken and Charlie talked for a few minutes. I saw Ken glance in my direction before telling Charlie he wanted to check up on his automobile insurance because he was thinking about moving to Montana where an army buddy said he could find a job. I felt myself flush. I turned back to my desk and tried to concentrate on my work. It was no use. I kept my head down, but listened to the men's conversation.

In answer to more questions from Charlie, Ken said he planned to move in a few weeks, adding that his mother was unhappy about his decision. He shook this head, saying there sure wasn't much happening around here.

Charlie checked Ken's file and told him his policy was paid up until the end of November. "You can renew that today, and you will be covered while you get settled in Montana. I'll look up the Montana regulations and send the information you need by mail."

All too soon I heard Charlie say goodbye. I turned for a final look at Ken and smiled. He answered with a heart-stopping smile before leaving. I watched him drive away and sighed . . . Ooooooh.

At the supper table that evening, I told my roommates about the handsome guy who had been in the office that afternoon and lamented the fact that he was moving to Montana. "All the good ones move away," commented one roommate.

Since none of us had any real plans for that evening, we lingered and exchanged stories about the men we were seeing and about those we had broken off with.

I laughed about one of my recent dates. My boss called me Susie after the secretary in the TV series *Private Secretary*—which was on TV from 1953 to 1957. When my date came to call for our second date, the girls told him there was no one by that name. I had to confess that I had given him a false name. Needless to say, I never saw him again.

My current boyfriend was one that a friend had introduced me to. We had a date Saturday night, back to the bar scene which I was getting a little tired of. I was getting tired of him too, although he seemed to want to get serious. I thought about Ken and sighed again. If only he wasn't moving to Montana.

The following Monday morning I had started to type the stack of invoices on my desk when a truck from Schroeder Greenhouse & Flower Shop in Green Bay stopped in front of the office. The driver came into the office and placed a glass vase with a bouquet of white carnations on the counter.

My boss read the card and set the flowers on my desk. "For you," he said.

I looked at my boss, then at the card.

"To a lovely girl with the unforgettable smile," it read and was signed "Ken".

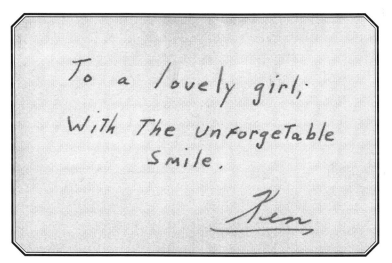

My emotions flew from excitement to a warm glow. I had never received flowers from anyone.

"Nice family," said Charlie. "Too bad he's leaving the state." My boss had been as surprised as I was by the flowers (by the way, I still have the vase).

I found Ken's address in the agency files and sent him a thank-you note. I wondered if he would reply and how long I would have to wait.

He called the next afternoon and offered me a ride home from work. I was flabbergasted. When I explained that I lived behind the agency where I worked, he suggested picking me up when my workday was over. "I'd like to see you again," he said.

"I get done at five . . . I'd like to see you too. Yes."

I was closing up the office when I saw his car drive up. I stayed back, taking the opportunity to gawk at him unnoticed while he walked toward the front door. Just as he got to the top step, I opened the door, turned and grinned at my boss, said good-bye, and closed the door behind me.

Nervous beyond words to be in such close proximity to this gorgeous hunk of a man, I smiled shyly at him. He returned a dazzling smile and I was a goner.

Ken spent that first day showing me the countryside around Green Bay. We stopped at Wequiock Falls, a small roadside park northeast of Green Bay. As we explored the grounds and walked along a narrow bridge above the waterfall, he told me about his family. He was the youngest of three children. Dorothy, the younger of his two sisters, had two girls, Denise and Lynn. Ginny, his older sister, had four children: one boy, Scott, and three girls, Karen, Christine, and Paula.

When he paused, I looked up at him and for a moment, he appeared lost in thought. He told me how his father had died of cancer when he was eighteen. He said he had the best father in the world but he felt that he had never really appreciated his dad when he was growing up. From what I had observed so far, I found that hard to believe.

When he asked me about my family, I answered without hesitation that I had none.

"No family?" he asked.

I didn't answer immediately. We walked on without speaking. After a while I said, "I don't know my family . . . I was raised in an orphanage."

"Oh," he said. "Oh."

He didn't ask any more questions, and I didn't volunteer any more information. I told him about my job and about graduating from St. Joseph Academy. He said he'd graduated from Central Catholic High School. I liked that; it meant we probably had our religion in common. He mentioned that he had served in the Army in Korea, but didn't elaborate any further. When he dropped me off at my apartment, he asked if he could see me the next day. "Yes," I answered, trying not to sound overly anxious.

For the next few hours, I don't think my feet touched the ground once. I think I pinched myself a few times. *Did I just have a date with the nicest, most heavenly guy I have ever seen? And was I actually going to see him again tomorrow? Maybe a lot of tomorrows?*

When Ken picked me up on Wednesday, he drove out into the country again. He stopped by the side of a road and pointed to a white house set back with long sweeping lawns, ringed by gardens of plantings and colorful flowers. I had never seen anything so peaceful. "That's what I'd like someday," he said looking right at me.

Thursday evening we went to a restaurant, then to a park and just talked. On Friday, he parked out at Austin Straubel Airfield (located in the village of Ashwaubenon, on the outskirts of Green Bay, now Austin Straubel International Airport). We talked for a long time, stopping to watch planes take off and land. He kissed me gently, and I kissed him back. While cuddling in the front seat of his car, he told me he wanted me to meet his family. I was surprised at this invitation. I had never received one like it before. And this soon! Did a boy take a girl home to meet his family after just four dates?

I spent Saturday morning deciding what to wear and worrying about what to say. Ken was picking me up at one o'clock in the afternoon. I wondered if he had told his mother and sisters about the orphanage. I wondered what their reaction had been.

As soon as we walked in the house, his sisters started teasing Ken. "You should have seen him the day he met you," said Dorothy. "He danced Mother around the kitchen." And his mother was happy that there was no more talk about moving to Montana.

From that Saturday onward, we spent nearly every day together, mostly at his mother's house. One weekend we drove up to Door County to see the glorious fall colors and stopped for ice cream. In the winter, we walked around his neighborhood, especially during or after a fresh snowfall, holding hands. Just the two of us, alone in a sparkling new world. I thought I was the luckiest girl alive.

In the months that followed, I fell more and more in love. My letters to Janet were filled with news of Ken. In the spring of 1956, Janet, with husband Rob, made a visit to Green Bay from Mississippi. Janet wanted to meet the man she had heard so much about.

We went out for an evening of dinner and dancing. I wore a dress I had made for special occasions: blue velvet with fitted bodice, full skirt, and white cashmere trim on the collar and sleeves.

The dress worked its magic. Ken kept his eyes on me all evening. During one particularly slow dance, he held me tight and whispered, "Oh, if we were married, you'd be in trouble tonight."

Shortly thereafter, Ken proposed. We began planning a summer wedding for the following year.

I felt the cracks in my shell grow wider and wider. Some pieces even broke off. I seldom gave thought anymore to Joan or my other siblings.

Then, out of the blue, in May of 1956, Joan called and my world was turned upside down.

CHAPTER TWENTY FIVE

May 1956
The Call

O ne of my roommates answered the ringing phone.
        "Hello." And after a pause: "No, let me get her."
"Hello." I said.
"Beatrice?"
"Yes." I didn't recognize the voice.
"This is your sister."
"What?"
"This is your sister, Joan," the voice repeated.

My heart skipped a beat—several, in fact. I must have stopped breathing for a full minute. This had to be someone's idea of a cruel joke. But I hadn't told anyone about my sister. I finally found my voice.

"Joan?" was all that came out.
"Yes. I want to see you."

I attempted to put a face with the voice. *When was the last time I saw my sister?*

"I have so much to tell you," the voice went on.
I think it was after Ellen came to the house.
"I need to see you." The voice was pleading.
Was it the day I had to go to court?
"Please." The voice entreated.
No, I didn't see her that day. Ellen said Joan had to talk to the judge later. I was there to testify because I was the only one at home when my mother made the threat. I didn't see Joan till the next day.

"You need to know what happened to me." The voice quivered. "Can we get together?"

The silence that followed was such that I could hear her breathing. "Who are you? Is this a joke?"

"This is no joke," she said. "It's really me. Please. Can we meet somewhere?"

Numb, that's what I was. The voice on the telephone was trying to convince me that she was the sister I had long ago given up hope of ever seeing again.

"How did you find me?"

"Not on the phone . . . I'll tell you everything."

Silence again. "Okay, but not here. I work every day till five."

"I'll pick you up tomorrow at five."

"OK . . . Yeah . . . All right."

My roommate asked what was wrong as I sank into one of the two chairs that took up most of the space in our kitchenette. I dismissed the question with a wave of my hand. I needed time to think.

Was that Joan on the phone? No one knew about my sister, not my roommates, not even Ken, my fiancé.

Would I recognize Joan? She was nine the last time I saw her, how long was that now? Fourteen years? I didn't know where she had been all this time. Tomorrow I'd find out. I wasn't sure I wanted to.

CHAPTER TWENTY SIX

May – August 1942
Joan – The Assault

The decision to wait for my sister outside the insurance agency office rather than in my apartment was an easy one. I knew my roommates would have many questions about her that I wasn't ready to answer.

When a car pulled up to the curb, the young woman emerging from the vehicle had a certain familiarity, something about her smile. She walked toward me, arms outstretched. I tensed up, pulled away, averting her eyes. After a few awkward moments, she said, "Let's get something to eat."

She drove to a west side restaurant; I remember we sat in a booth. I looked hard into her face. Only seconds passed before I realized that this was indeed the sister I thought had died. She told me she was married and had three children.

"I guess that makes me an aunt." I smiled at her.

After the waitress took our order, I leaned back against the Naugahyde cushion. "What happened? Where did you go? Where have you been?" My head was swirling with questions.

Joan began by telling me she was sorry for not contacting me sooner but she had her reasons. She said she hoped I could forgive her and that I would understand after I heard everything. We sat not speaking for a few minutes. I think Joan was trying to compose herself. When she started to speak again, her voice was shaky.

"I've never been able to forget that day. It was in 1942, the beginning of May. It was early; you kids weren't up yet. When there was a knock on the front door, Glenda went to answer it."

"Why do you call her Glenda?" I asked.

"Because that's her name and I can't think of anything else to call her."

I told Joan I was sorry for interrupting and to please continue.

"I followed Glenda and saw a nice-looking young man standing on our porch. I was standing behind her and I heard him say, 'I'm Carl Janquet. Father Thomas asked me to come see you. I believe we met at church.'"

Joan said she didn't believe her mother remembered Carl because Glenda was frowning. "She asked me if I remembered Carl. I told her I'd never seen him before. When he smiled at me, I got prickles on the back of my neck. When Glenda asked what he wanted, Carl told her that Father Thomas wanted him to talk to me.

"Glenda wanted to know 'What for?' She was still frowning, more like squinting. The sun was in her eyes.

"'About her grandfather,' he answered. I stepped around to stand by the door beside my mother. She asked Carl why Father wanted him to talk to me about my grandfather. He said Father had gotten some reports that my grandfather was an alcoholic and a child abuser.

"Glenda looked confused, didn't say anything for a minute, then she said that it might not be such a bad idea to get the business about grandpa settled once and for all. She thought the park would be a good place to talk.

"I told her I couldn't, that I had to go to school. She told me I could skip school and insisted I go with Carl."

Just then, the waitress arrived with our food and as soon as she was gone I asked, "What business about grandpa?"

"Glenda didn't want to allow him to come to our house anymore. There was a lot of gossip among our relatives . . . I wasn't the only one he did it to."

"Did what to?"

"He liked little girls. Couldn't keep his hands off of them."

"Oh, my God!"

"Please tell me he never touched you."

"No, he didn't."

Joan sounded relieved when she said, "Hmmmm . . . Let's eat. I'm starved."

After a few bites, she pushed her plate away and started talking again.

"There weren't any people in the park; it was early. I stayed ahead of Carl. He looked around before walking to the edge of the kiddie pool. He invited me to sit there with him, but I told him I was afraid of the water.

"He laughed. 'Not this water. The pool is shallow at this end. I'll show you.' He removed his shoes and socks, rolled up his pant legs, and waded to the pool. 'See, my knees aren't even wet.'

"He got out of the water and rolled down his pant legs. I walked away from him. I thought he was acting strange.

"'Come on,' he suddenly said behind me. He touched my shoulder. I followed him, but walked far enough away that he couldn't touch me again."

Joan stopped talking and looked at me. Her face was pale. I was beginning to get the picture and felt uncomfortable. The burger and fries I had ordered no longer looked appetizing. I asked Joan why she didn't run home.

"Well, he changed then, and he asked how I was doing in school. But he didn't wait for my answer. Instead, he ducked behind a low-hanging willow tree. I thought he was playing a game, but before I could decide if I should follow, he yanked me under the branches and opened the front of his trousers. He wiggled his stiff penis at me. He grabbed my hair, dragged me toward him, and thrust himself into my mouth. He ejaculated, and I gagged on his semen. When he pushed me away, I landed hard, choking and coughing, on the ground.

"He grabbed my hair a second time. 'Don't tell anyone what happened here today,' he said, 'or I'll come back and drown you in the pool. Besides, no one will believe you.' He straightened his clothes and strode off."

By now I was sure I had wandered into someone else's nightmare. "What did you do?" I asked.

"I ran home as fast as I could, up the stairs to the bedroom, and crawled under the bed. I was so scared. I could hear the mice in the room but I had to hide. I was more afraid of Carl finding me than I was of the mice. Glenda must have heard the door slam. I could hear her lumbering up the stairs; she was about six months pregnant. She asked me what happened. I didn't answer. I crawled out and sat next to her, pulled my dress over my head, and sobbed."

The waitress, noticing we hadn't finished our food, came over and asked if everything was okay. We assured her that it was and sat silently while we ate. When we finished, Joan asked if I'd like to go someplace else. I could see that she was visibly shaken. I told her, "Yes, I would."

"There's a nice quiet park near downtown, Astor Park on Porlier Street. We'll have more privacy there." She paid the bill and we left the restaurant.

On the way to Astor Park, Joan told me she had tried to contact me. "In 1954," she said. "But I chickened out. I didn't know what I'd say to you." Not waiting for my questions, she said, "I'll tell you about that another time."

We sat at a picnic table in the park near some large trees. Joan showed me pictures of her husband and children before getting back to her story.

"Glenda knew something was wrong," Joan began. "I think she also knew it had to do with Carl. She wanted to know how her 'sunny and outgoing' daughter could change so suddenly to 'glum and sulky.'

"By the middle of July, Glenda said she'd had enough. She hadn't told anyone about her fear that I had been assaulted. Two months was long enough to live with the lie. She said she was going to talk to Father Thomas and ask him about Carl. She left you kids with a neighbor and took me with her.

"He denied knowing Carl; said he'd never heard of him. She told him not to hand her any of that crap. 'You know who he is. Carl Janquet. You sent him over to my house. He molested my daughter.'

"When Father Thomas asked what he should do about it, she answered him in an angry voice, 'Investigate Carl, ask him what he did to my daughter, have him arrested.'

"Father Thomas said he couldn't do that because he had no idea what she was talking about. Glenda was furious.

"'Then how did Carl know about Joan being molested by her grandfather?'

"They were talking like I wasn't even there. He said a lot of people knew about my grandfather. Anyone could have told him."

I could see that Joan was becoming unnerved. It was getting late and I was meeting Ken. I couldn't take any more right now. I suggested we continue another day. Joan replied, "Yes." She said she had to relieve her mother-in-law from baby-sitting.

She dropped me off at my apartment. As I was getting out of the car, she touched my hand and said she'd call me. I smiled and turned away.

CHAPTER TWENTY SEVEN

September 1942
Joan – The Interrogation

Joan and I met a few weeks later, again at the park. She brought along a picnic basket. She opened the basket, unfolded a red checkered tablecloth, placed it on the table, and spread out the picnic lunch—egg-salad sandwiches, apples, chocolate chip cookies, and cokes—between us. She talked about her growing family, said she was expecting again. I told her I was engaged, talked a little bit about Ken. She was excited for me, wanted to meet Ken. I said okay, soon. I didn't tell her that I had not yet told Ken about her.

I started by asking Joan if she knew what happened after Edward was born. "The day after Glenda came home with him, the three younger kids were still at the farm. You were gone to the store. The caseworker came to the house to talk to Glenda, and I had to testify in court about a threat she made."

Joan said, "Yes," she'd heard about all that.

"Mmmm, good sandwiches," I piped in. "Homemade cookies?"

"My mother-in-law made them," she answered.

"You know," she said, getting serious again, "I had to testify too. The judge asked me about grandpa and stuff about home."

"I remember I saw you the next day," I said. "That was the last time."

"Yeah, Glenda sent you to the park because she didn't want you to be there when the caseworker picked me up."

"I remember. I asked her that night where you were, but she wouldn't tell me. Where did you go?"

"I had to go to Father Henri's office. He wanted to talk to me. You know, after the court hearing, we were in the custody of the Green Bay Diocese Apostolate."

The Green Bay Diocese Apostolate, with an office in Green Bay, provided casework services to the orphanage. Since the majority of children were referred by the Apostolate, the staff at the institution relied on the Apostolate caseworkers for direction in determining the care and services the institution was to provide. Father Henri, director of the Apostolate, working with a small staff, personally acquainted himself with many of the children in the orphanage and their families.

In April of 1942, the family's situation was brought to Father Henri's attention. By August, everything had come to a head.

"It was late in the afternoon," Joan continued, "when we arrived at Father Henri's office. It was September first. I'll never forget that day either. He had the caseworker wait in the outer office. He asked me a lot of the same questions the judge had. It was like an inquisition."

"'How often were you alone with your grandfather?' he asked. I told him I hadn't seen my grandfather in a long time because my mother wouldn't let him come to our house anymore."

"He asked, 'Why, what did your grandfather do to you?' I told Father Henri that my grandfather hugged me a lot and patted me all over."

"'Did he take your clothes off?' Father asked."

"'Sometimes,' I answered."

"'Did he make you touch him?'"

"'Yes.'"

"'Did you tell him to stop?'"

"'No. I was afraid of him.'"

We finished our lunch. Joan packed everything back into the picnic basket. We made small talk about the park and the sunny day while we sipped our Cokes. I could see that she was upset.

When she continued, she confided that she didn't think Father Henri believed anything about the Carl Janquet story.

"He asked me if I had ever seen Carl before, maybe in church?"

"I told him 'No,' I hadn't."

"'Why did you go to the park with him?' he asked.

"'My mother said I should,' I answered. "'He said Father Thomas wanted him to talk to me about my grandfather.'

"I know that priest didn't believe me because he said, 'Did he talk to you about your grandfather?' and I said 'No.'

"He wanted to know what we did talk about. I told him I didn't remember. Just that I was afraid of the water, that Carl took his shoes and socks off and waded into the pool. After he put his shoes and socks back on, he went behind the tree and pulled me by the hair.

"Father Henri's expression didn't change one bit when I told him the rest, about Carl opening his fly, putting his thing in my mouth, and threatening to drown me. He only asked me if I told my mother and I said, 'No.'"

"'Then how did she know?' he asked. I had no answer for that one."

"Then he had the nerve to ask me if I was sure that it was Carl who did those things to me and not my grandfather.

"'No, it was Carl.'

"That was when Father Henri got up from his chair and walked over to the door, leaving me squirming in my chair. He called the caseworker into his office, sat down, leaned forward, and said to me, 'Listen dear, we can't have you to talking to other children about this.'

"He looked at the caseworker and said, 'She'll have to spend the night at the orphanage. Have Sister Agatha keep her out of sight. And get the rest of the kids out of that house.'"

I was having a difficult time digesting all that Joan had told me, as much for the horror as for the sadness that had deprived us of growing up together. I sensed Joan's contempt whenever she mentioned Glenda's name. I asked Joan if she thought there was a cover-up, but she said there was no way of knowing or proving it.

There was so much more to talk about, but my brain was spinning. I needed time to let this all sink in. I was exhausted, as I'm sure Joan was. We agreed we would get together again in a few weeks.

CHAPTER TWENTY EIGHT

September 1942
Joan – Committed

"After questioning me," Joan began the next time we got together early that summer, "Father Henri said to take me directly to the orphanage.

"When we got there, Sister Agatha told another nun to put me up in one of the guest bedrooms for the night. 'The smaller room with one bed,' she said. 'She's to be here overnight and not to talk to any other children.'

"I was so tired I took off my shoes, lay down on the bed, and fell asleep. When I woke up, it took me a few minutes to realize where I was. I wondered what I would tell you when I got home. I worried about you, more since you had fallen.

"I didn't have time to think of much else. Sister Agatha came in, told me to put my shoes on, and hustled me out to a waiting car. The caseworker, the same one as the day before, drove me to Good Shepherd's Home. I don't know how many months I was there before they found a foster home for me."

I didn't think this was a good time to tell Joan I had also been at Good Shepherd's. That was another experience I had buried very deep. It was too painful to think about.

Joan was talking again. "While at Good Shepherd's, the Apostolate ordered weekly counseling sessions for me with Father Henri. We talked about all kinds of things, but the priest seemed most concerned about my knowing the difference between lying and telling the truth. I didn't understand his concern or the reasons for the counseling. I didn't know what I had done wrong."

Joan's story overwhelmed me. I had a difficult time focusing on what she was saying. Every new revelation only raised more questions. Why had she taken this long to contact me? When we were children, all we'd had was each other.

When I asked her if she knew what happened to our younger siblings after they left the orphanage, she said she knew that Joe and Ann had gone to a foster home together. "To a farm, to be nothing more than 'work horses,'" she added.

I asked her how she had found me. She shrugged, seemed reluctant, and said she didn't remember who told her. Maybe one of the caseworkers she'd had to deal with. "I think I had a different worker for every new foster home I went to. I called the last one I had talked to. I think she's the one who helped me find you."

CHAPTER TWENTY NINE

1945
Joan – Crying Out

J oan and I met several times over the next few weeks. She told me nobody listened to Glenda when she went into a rage demanding justice for her daughter. All they told her was that they didn't know anyone named Carl.

"I don't know if you know this," Joan said the last time we got together that summer, "but Glenda moved to Chicago after her divorce and got married again, to a man she met in a bar."

I told her I knew Glenda had moved to Chicago; that I had gotten a few letters from her at the orphanage, and yes, she had a different last name.

Joan continued. "There are some things you need to know about this woman who was our mother.

"In 1945, after she got married, she gained custody of me. While I was living with her, she told me she wanted to have another baby. I thought that was disgusting. She said that when the Apostolate took us away she told them she would never allow us to be adopted, that 'we didn't need the world with a fence around it.'

"I didn't see much of Glenda and her new husband. I attended school every day and survived by begging for rides, borrowing clothes, and charming food from my classmates.

"One night Glenda coaxed me into accompanying her, her husband, and some friends, barhopping. In the early morning hours, when everyone was drunk, they piled into a car to go home. I was forced to sit on a man's lap. He fondled me, first my breasts, then my thighs. I remembered Carl and my grandfather and it made me sick to my stomach. I didn't say anything; I thought that would make matters worse.

"After a few months, Glenda's husband left and then she left. I was all alone in Chicago. With the $6.00 that Glenda had given me, I took the train back to Green Bay, where the authorities found me another foster home.

"I was in six different foster homes, five in Green Bay and one in Wittenberg. I was with two different families in Green Bay before Glenda got me. I was with one family in Green Bay when I graduated from eighth grade and another one when I attended St. Joseph Academy for my freshman year. I was in Wittenberg for my sophomore year and back in Green Bay for my junior and part of my senior year.

"Halfway through my senior year, I wanted to get a job. A clerk at the Brown County Courthouse told me that to get a work permit, I needed my birth certificate and wrote down where I had to go to get it. St. Mary's Mothers and Infants' Home.

"When I got to the Home, I rang the bell and a nun opened a sliding door and asked what I wanted. I told her I was there to get my birth certificate and gave her my last name. She told me to stand outside and wait. After a long while, she returned and said there was no birth certificate with that name but that she had found mine. She passed the certificate through the sliding door and that's when I found out what my mother had done. The space for a father's name was blank. It read 'Illegitimate.' I was devastated."

I don't know if Joan saw the color drain from my face. I let her continue talking.

She went on about how angry she became. How that anger fueled rebellion and the rebellion lead to a move to the Good Shepherd's Home. "I spent the last three months of my senior year there. One of the sisters took me under her wing and offered me guidance during those months.

"I considered becoming a nun, but when I confided in Sister Superior, she placed her hands on my shoulders and said, 'Oh no dear, you could never be one of us.' I wasn't good enough.

"Later, when Glenda tried to contact me, I made it clear I wanted nothing more to do with her. I was brokenhearted when I found out that you were my half-sister, and that I was a bastard. I'll have to admit I wasn't too surprised, given how Harold had treated me.

"I deliberately did not attempt to contact you because I was sure Glenda would try to get to me through you. I didn't want to run into her. I'd escaped her and she couldn't hurt me anymore. I also felt bad, and guilty, that I had not invited you to my wedding.

"What I was really afraid of," Joan continued, "was that you would expect more from me than I had to give. I often thought about you. I took care of you when you were little. You loved it when I read to you. I wondered what kind of adult you had grown into. I felt it was time for you to know what happened to me."

I felt my shell reforming, the cracks closing up. I heard my sister say she was sorry, I said I was sorry too, but could we get together again some other time. I saw the sadness in her face when I told her I had to get home.

I knew there was no way to make Joan understand what I was feeling. I had long ago been reconciled to the fact that I had no family and that she was gone. And now to find out she could have contacted me but didn't, and that we were half-sisters. Why did she have to come back into my life now that I was settling down and getting married?

Would things have been different if we had been together in the orphanage? Could Joan have protected me from Sister Edythe, or from the assaults?

What about now? Joan and I were strangers to each other. We would have to become reacquainted. Could we learn to be friends again? What about our younger siblings? Where did they fit into Joan's and my life? Did they?

The only fact that was clear in my mind was that my childhood and my sister had been stolen from me, and the Apostolate was to blame for that. That agency had separated me from my sister, the one person I had needed as a child.

My shell reformed and hardened around the memories relating to the Apostolate. For the first time, I put a name to that shell. Unforgiveness. Would I ever find the ability to forgive the people who had done this to us?

CHAPTER THIRTY

1957
Green Bay
Happiness at Last

Torn between my past and my future, between Joan and the feelings my sister resurrected, and my love for Ken, I had to choose. If I focused on my sister, I felt my shell begin squeezing the breath out of me. If I focused on my fiancé, I felt the shell loosen its grip. My priority had to be Ken and the future we were creating.

I openly adored him. He was a down-to-earth, good, and honest man with a subtle sense of humor. His large hands were strong but gentle; they had built steel Quonset huts in the cold Korean hills, but could tenderly stroke his pet parakeet's soft blue feathers. About serious things, such as his faith, his family, and our future, he was serious.

Sometimes while sitting across from him in his mother's kitchen, I'd gaze at his beautiful face and I had to remind myself that I got to touch that face and kiss that mouth. I insisted on washing his thick lush hair just to run my fingers through it.

My wedding was months away and I was glad that Joan was in my life again. Our relationship at first was tentative. I don't think either of us knew how to be a sister to the other. But we promised we'd try. I had told Ken about her without revealing too much information. I made it sound like Joan didn't know where I was all this time, which was true. Joan fell in love with Ken immediately. I asked her to be my matron of honor.

Our wedding took place on June 1, 1957, at St. Joseph's Catholic Church, a new parish on Twelfth Avenue in Green Bay. As I walked down the aisle, all

I saw was Ken, handsome as ever in his white jacket and shirt with black tie and black pants. And the way he said "Wow" when he saw me.

Joan hosted a wedding breakfast at her new home on the West side of Green Bay. Ken and I hosted a reception at the Chatterbox restaurant in De Pere.

We rented a one-bedroom, second-floor apartment near Ken's mother's home and transformed it with our own touches. The only access to the apartment was outdoor stairs. I had a small dowry of pots, pans, dishes, and linens persuasive salesmen had eagerly pushed on recent high school graduates. Ken's mother had given us a wooden four-chair dining set which we refinished

We settled into our apartment after a weekend honeymoon in Wisconsin's Door County, a popular area north of Green Bay (in Wisconsin's thumb, protruding out of Green Bay and Lake Michigan).

At last I had found love. The years ahead would be sweet.

I soon learned married life wasn't without its challenges. For one thing, I had to learn to cook. Plucking chickens, frosting hot cross buns, and exploding root beer didn't count. When I was single, I lived on hamburgers and the contents of Kellogg's cereal boxes.

To get started and to prevent any more mishaps, I purchased a cookbook: Meta Given's *Modern Encyclopedia of Cooking*. The two-volume, fifteen hundred-page cookbook covered every contingency from planning menus to shopping for fruits and vegetables, from measurement equivalencies to recognizing cuts of meat. Some of the more unusual entries included how to make sauerkraut, and how to cook some animals I'd rather not know about. There was a chapter on chickens, including graphics illustrating how chickens went from feathers to stockpot; I would buy my chickens ready for the pot. I started with simple recipes, pork chops and casseroles. Bouillabaisse and baked Alaska would come much later.

I was a workaholic perfectionist. The whole house groaned when I reached for a bucket or a polishing cloth. Only a fanatic would even think about covering a sofa and chair with plastic, but worse than that, take the covers off every spring just long enough to shampoo the furniture.

Shortly after we were married, Ken bought a Volkswagen Beetle. I got a kick out of watching my six-foot-two-inch husband climbing out of the vehicle. It was a sight to behold, like watching origami unfolding. First, his long legs emerged, then his head, and finally the rest of his body.

Ken did all the driving at first. I'd gotten my driver's license when I was sixteen driving an automatic shift. The time had come for me to learn to drive a stick shift. Ken was my teacher. The lessons took place around the neighborhood and in vacant parking lots. Until I became skilled, the rides were jerky stops and starts.

My first solo test occurred on an afternoon when I had to get freshly baked cookies to my parish bake sale by a 2:00 p.m. deadline. Ken was working nights then, and he was sleeping. I didn't want to wake him.

I can do this. I gritted my teeth and grabbed the car keys. Driving twenty miles an hour, I made it to the church. There was a moment at a stop sign when I wasn't sure I could make it across a busy intersection. But make it I did. None of the cookies slid on the floor or arrived broken. When I told Ken, he asked how I did it. "God might have helped," was my reply.

Two months after my marriage, while working at New York Life Insurance Company, I learned I was pregnant, due in May. Because New York Life required an expectant mother to quit her job well before the baby's birth, I left the workforce in December 1957.

I was excited and nervous about becoming a parent. With no mother/ child experience to fall back on, this would have to be a learn-as-you-go process. I read Dr. Spock, but in the end, I think I flunked parenthood.

As the birth grew closer, Ken and I moved into a two-bedroom apartment, again on an upper floor with outdoor stairs. Baby Kathy arrived on May 7, 1958, inheriting her father's good looks and my brown eyes. Often, after we put her to bed for the night, we'd stand over her crib and watch her sleep, and playfully nudged each other to see who could take more credit for the miracle that had come into our lives. A sweet, vivid memory for me was watching the two of them sound asleep on the couch, Kathy lying on her daddy's chest.

One of the challenges of new parenthood was laundry. My sister-in-law, Ginny, had given us a wringer washing machine when she purchased a new modern one. We couldn't afford to buy one, and I didn't relish the idea of washing everything by hand. The washer joined two laundry tubs, property of our landlady, in the basement of our apartment. Problem was, the tubs were also used as a bathtub for her Great Dane, and she didn't clean them after his bath. I'd have to scrub out the slime and dried-on hair before I could use them. My "dryer" consisted of clotheslines (hemp ropes) strung up in my ten-foot-by-ten-foot kitchen. Wooden clothespins held all the laundry, including the cloth diapers, in place.

Pregnant for the second time, due in April 1961, I wanted my own home. Ken and I chose a new neighborhood on Green Bay's west side. We had a three-bedroom house built for us, minus a garage; we were lucky to afford the house. The cost? $11,000. The house was about four blocks from the Green Bay Packers stadium, Lambeau Field. This was during the team's glory years when they won championships in 1961 and 1962, Super Bowl I in 1967, and Super Bowl II in 1968. Cars choked off the streets around the stadium. Sitting on our front porch, we could watch the fashion parade of fans go by.

The Packers' season was practically the highlight of the 1960s social life. Pre-game breakfasts, post-game dinners, local restaurants crowded, and women dressed to the nines for the game. Dressy outfits, high heels, and even on Indian summer days and unseasonably warm summer temperatures, fur coats were commonly seen in the stands.

My second daughter, Mary, was born on April 3, 1961. She grew to be the prettiest little girl with green eyes and blonde hair. She's the dancer in our family, tall with long, supple legs. When she was three, she was on Romper Room, a popular children's television series.

For both of my girls, this was a time of roller skates, bicycles, hula-hoops, and dance classes. In the summer, they played ball with Ken and swam in their baby pool. In the winter, they helped their father shovel snow, each with their own baby shovel. There were birthday parties with fancy cakes, and trips to the Reforestation Camp in Suamico to feed the deer. I sewed the girls' clothes, often dressed them alike. They got the frilly bedroom I had longed for as a child.

My son Paul, named for Ken's father, was born on December 14, 1964. He was the spittin' image of Ken, his daddy's boy. People couldn't resist picking him up. He was so cute, had the softest skin, the biggest brown eyes, and Ken's endearing smile. Now Ken had a boy that he could rough and tumble with, and the girls had a baby brother they could spoil.

Our lifestyle was typical of a family in the 1960s. We participated in school and church projects. Kathy and Mary were in Brownies and Kathy in Girl Scouts. Young families primarily made up our neighborhood. There were picnics and block parties galore, some recorded on silent film. For a pet, we adopted a parakeet, named it McGee, and taught it to say, "Pretty bird." (I stole that whole idea from my foster parents, the Joneses.)

The best times were Ken's family gatherings, especially Christmas, exchanging presents, visiting his uncles. His aunts made the best cookies.

Ginny added three more children to her family: Eileen, Dianne, and Jeff. Dorothy added two: Paul and John.

Being part of Ken's family was about love and simplicity of life.

But all was not perfect. I was a formidable disciplinarian with my kids. My perfectionism and rigidity got in the way one day and sent me over the edge.

Kathy was around eighteen months old. I went to get her from her nap and found her in her crib, naked, and completely covered with the brown contents of her diaper. Parts of the wall and every rail and spindle on her bed were smeared with dried-on baby poop. I thought about all the time it was going to take me to clean up the mess, and I lost control. I got a wooden spoon from the kitchen and spanked her baby's bottom again and again.

Listening to Kathy's cries, I realized the magnitude of what I'd done. Never again, I promised myself, and put the spoon away. I cleaned up my daughter and put her back in bed. I never hit any of my kids like that again. Ground them, make them stand in corners, yes; hit them, no. One thing I regret not doing that day was holding my daughter and giving her a long, loving hug. Shame on me.

Another part of my past that seemed inescapable was Glenda. Like my sister Joan, I had decided long ago that I wanted nothing to do with her. One summer afternoon, when I was outside in my driveway watching my daughters splash around in their plastic, round swimming pool, a car drove up. Glenda emerged and walked up to the girls.

"Hi. I'm your grandmother," she said.

Caught off guard, I snapped, "No, you're not. They only have one grandmother."

She looked around at the exterior of my house, then my growing belly; I was pregnant with Paul. "Don't have so many children," she advised before turning back to her car.

That statement was too much for me. I didn't need the likes of this woman telling me how to run my life when her own had been such a mess. She was the one who wanted to have as many babies as she could without taking responsibility for raising them. She was the one who had been too proud to let her children be adopted.

My voice had a hard edge to it when I told my mother I preferred that she not try to contact me again.

The 1950s brought us Elvis, the Korean War, and polio vaccine (I remember everyone being afraid to take their children anywhere for fear they would get the disease). Very short hairstyles were fashionable while dresses were longer. Hats were *the* thing, and a lady never went anywhere without her white gloves. Harry S. Truman and Dwight D. Eisenhower were our presidents. Bing Crosby, Bob Hope, Frank Sinatra, and Marilyn Monroe entertained us. I remember going to see *Gone With the Wind* in 1954 and being surprised that it had had its premiere showing in 1939. In 1950 you could buy a new house for $8,450; by 1959, the same house cost $12,400. A new car went from $1,510 to $2,200, and a gallon of gas went from 18 cents to 25 cents.

It was a simpler time, after the war. Families ate together and went to church together. Most moms stayed home to look after the kids while dads went to work. If you disrespected a teacher or an adult neighbor, you were grounded or punished. It was an age of innocence, and nothing has been the same since.

Looking back on my marriage after nine and a half years, I felt my life, while not perfect, could not have been more blessed, nor Ken in his quiet way more wonderful. My shell was nearly gone, and I looked forward to a future that was equally blissful

CHAPTER THIRTY ONE

1966
Green Bay
God Giveth and God Taketh Away

October 17, 1966, a day burned in my memory. Ken came home early from his shift at National Can Company. He said he didn't feel well but didn't say much more; like most men, he wasn't one to talk about his health. He went into the bathroom. A minute later, I heard what sounded like coughing or choking. I quickly phoned the doctor.

By the time I opened the bathroom door to check on Ken, he was slumped over on his knees. Frantic, I called my neighbors, Bill and Mary Falk, from across the street for help. They rushed over and Bill gave Ken mouth-to-mouth resuscitation until the doctor arrived.

After examining Ken for what seemed like a better part of eternity, the doctor stood up and said, "There's nothing more I can do for him."

"Why not?" I asked, thinking the doctor meant that there was nothing more he could do at our home, that Ken would have to go to the hospital emergency room.

"Because he's dead," the doctor answered.

"Oh . . . n-o-o-o-o," I moaned falling against the nearest wall. I'm not clear what happened after that. Some of it I learned later.

The Falks took charge. Bill and the doctor moved Ken's body to our bedroom and laid it on the bed. Mary called Ken's sisters and they both came to the house. They waited until morning to tell their mother. I can't imagine the anguish she must have gone through when she learned her only son was dead. They wouldn't let me see Ken. The doctor gave me medication to make me sleep. I didn't sleep.

My sister-in-law, Dorothy, helped with the funeral arrangements. The doctor decided it was not necessary to have an autopsy; he didn't want to put the family through that ordeal. Ken had been diagnosed with rheumatic fever (an inflammatory disease caused by strep throat) in 1960. Complications from that disease were responsible for his death. He had just turned thirty-four.

I was not prepared for what lay ahead. I had not seen Ken since finding him in the bathroom, so I let myself believe that the last few days had not happened. I walked into the Blaney Funeral parlor knowing this was a place where I did not want to be. Then I saw him, and I had to face the fact that the person lying in the casket was my husband.

"It can't be. It can't be," I cried.

I managed to cross the room with my eight-year-old daughter. Kathy stepped up on the kneeler in front of the casket and tried to open her father's eyes. I gazed at the beautiful person lying there as though he were asleep, his big gentle hands crossed in front of his body. I would never again see his smile or be able to run my fingers through his hair. I would miss his big silly grin when he was sure he had told a funny joke—that nobody got. I couldn't watch him ride his daughter's bike with his long legs sticking up above the handlebars, or watch him tumble with our son.

Friends and family offered condolences, expressed concern for the children. I don't remember acknowledging any of them.

The Funeral Mass was held at our parish, St. Agnes, on Ninth Street, and he was buried in Allouez Catholic cemetery.

I couldn't accept Ken's death or his funeral and, least of all, his burial. How would I survive without him? How would the children manage without their father? I wanted to pull him from the cold earth, wrap my arms around his body, and bring him back to life. But I couldn't.

Some weeks later, after my children were in bed, I paced the house, wandered from room to room, and caressed the things Ken had used, things we had shared. I worried about the kids. They needed their father. What kind of future could I give them?

I stopped pacing, stood in the middle of the living room, looked up at the ceiling, and screamed, "Why did you do this to me, God?"

Even sleep brought me no rest. I had recurring dreams about Ken. He was mine again. Then some stranger—always someone different—appeared, and claimed him. Ken tried to get back to me, but I could never quite reach him.

The dreams were so vivid that at night, I couldn't wait for sleep to come. Maybe I'd have one more minute with my husband.

In spite of my quarrel with God, I continued the relationship with my church, believing it to be paramount in my children's upbringing. They would attend their parish school, receive the sacraments, celebrate holydays, and go to Mass. As for me, I would remain angry with God. As a matter of fact, I had begun to question the existence of God.

That anger took the form of a new shell, thicker and tighter than the old one. For a long time, I didn't care.

Ken's family supported me through months of grieving. My existence was simply getting through one day at a time while trying to give my children the care they needed.

The wife of one of Ken's friends, who had lost her husband to Hodgkin's disease, called one day and invited me to join a singles group. I went once, but was not yet ready to see people.

Then about a year and a half later, I joined the group for things like bowling, volleyball, dancing, swimming at the YMCA, and plays at St. Norbert College.

My neighbors continued to be supportive friends, inviting me to some of the block parties. One such party occurred in February 1969. The neighbor planning the affair—a "bored-with-winter" party—told me she had invited a blind date for me, a guy by the name of Jerry Seidl who had lost his wife to cancer, and deemed it necessary to include the gentleman's resume.

"He lives in De Pere. He's a lot of fun, but he's not for you. He has five kids."

That was one prognostication that would more than prove false.

CHAPTER THIRTY TWO

February 1969
De Pere, Wisconsin
Another Chance

My neighbor had talked so much about Jerry, what he looked like and how he dressed, that I knew him immediately when he arrived at the party. I was in the basement recreation room with other neighbors when he began descending the stairs. First into view were his black cowboy boots, then his pants, which were a bit too short. A belt with a large, shiny cowboy buckle held his pants in place. A big head of curly hair topped off a pair of twinkling hazel eyes

"He makes quite a first impression," I said to her.

"I told you so," she laughed.

The second, third, and fourth impressions equaled and even surpassed the first. He was a barrel of fun, laughing and joking with everyone. He had the wit of a stand-up comic—said he'd played one in high school. He never stopped talking, and he loved to dance, two things not unnoticed by me, since I was Spartan at the first, and bewitched by the second. Call it intrigue, but he was the exact opposite of my sweet, quiet Ken. When he walked me home after the party, he asked if he could see me again, and that was that.

What I discovered about Jerry was that he was a man of many talents and a fast worker. We began going together almost immediately. A musician who played guitar, accordion, harmonica, piano, and organ, he phoned me every night, and one time I could hear organ music in the background. He was playing me love songs, Beatles stuff: "Yesterday," "Hey Jude," "Let It Be."

Jerry introduced me to his parents, Mae and Curly, and his five children: Barbara, eleven; Lynn, nine; Pam, seven; Julie, five; and Patrick, four. He met my three: Kathy, ten; Mary, seven; and Paul, four. This was about the time I insisted people call me by the shortened version of my name.

In April 1969, three months after we met, we began talking about marriage. It was an understanding. There was no formal proposal, and he did not give me an engagement ring. We mutually agreed not to adopt each other's children and that eight was enough.

Jerry and I began construction on a five-bedroom house in De Pere in May. We married in August, a year after Jerry's first wife died. Until the new house was scheduled to be finished—a month after the wedding—we crammed all ten of us in Jerry's three-bedroom house.

The lot that we had purchased for our colonial-style home was overgrown with weeds, bushes, and trees. We needed to get it cleared before the bulldozer came to dig the basement. Jerry cajoled some of his neighbors and friends to help us clear the land.

There we all were on a Saturday afternoon, pulling, digging, chopping, and dragging. And there I was, getting a nifty case of poison ivy. Where was Jerry? He was out front in the street doing what he did best: talking, telling jokes. Which meant that at any given moment, there were at least two people doing absolutely nothing.

After Jerry and I decided to marry, I volunteered to take over running his household, a job I soon would have anyway. My toughest challenge was his basement. As I rubbed calamine lotion on my poison ivy rash, I pondered how I would deal with the problem in such a way that Jerry would help solve it. I wanted to get into the basement and clean up the chaos that I knew existed there.

He told me that the basement was also where he worked on his hobbies and stored his collections. I wondered what he collected and how many hobbies he had. Whenever I mentioned the basement, Jerry changed the subject. I was starting to realize I'd have to stand my ground with him.

The next time the basement came up in discussion, Jerry put me off. "It's too messy. I'll take care of it."

A woman knows better. While a man may be sincere when he promises to undertake a project like cleaning the basement, he avoids setting an actual time or date for doing it. Even if he does, some male activity such as a Packers or Brewers game, bowling, or golf takes precedence. The woman is left with three choices—nagging until the promise is kept, doing it herself, or hiring outside help.

I had a fourth alternative in mind—the children. But first I wanted to see what I had to contend with. I insisted that he let me see the basement.

My jaw dropped as I descended the basement stairs. The first thing I saw was a mountain—we're talking *Everest* here—of clothes.

"What the hell are you people wearing?" I was dumbfounded. Jerry explained it was easier to go out and buy new clothes when the family ran out of clean ones than contend with the laundry.

"Don't you have a washer and dryer?" I asked. Jerry shrugged. He thought they were buried under the laundry. He went on to explain that before he met me, neighbors had helped with the laundry, but he hated to keep bothering them. I told him I would start on the laundry immediately.

Beyond the clothes were hundreds of glass wine bottles, some filled with beet or dandelion wine, some empty. He had written a book on the subject of winemaking. He had a couple boxes of those because, unfortunately, he had sold only two copies.

He liked to build things. That explained the wood stacked from floor to ceiling, some in the rafters, and some leaning against the basement walls, as well as the multiple tools and assorted cans of screws and nails. The rest of the basement was filled with every magazine he had ever read, newspapers, rolls of brown wrapping paper, reams of typing paper, and boxes of light bulbs. Here and there were boxes of "unknowns." He had taken electrical courses and installed sound systems. There were rolls and boxes of various wiring.

In one corner were bolts of fake fur fabric in tiger and zebra stripes. Jerry had used the fabric to cover speakers he built for Henri's Music Store. The speaker venture fizzled, and the fabric gathered dust in the basement.

I looked at the disorder around me, squared my shoulders, and summoned the children as soon as I returned upstairs. I told them we had to have all the "junk" at the curb on the city's rubbish pickup day.

Jerry was reduced to watching helplessly as most of his "treasure" marched its way to the curb into oblivion. He had no choice since he was out-numbered, nine to one. Chalk one up for Bea.

I saved the fabric.

The morning of our wedding I showered, dressed, and left my house in Green Bay for the last time. As I drove south into De Pere, I spotted Jerry going in the opposite direction, north to Green Bay. His parents, who had also seen him, later told me they thought he had changed his mind.

In fact, Jerry had gone to find his one and only suit. I had taken it to the dry cleaners, picked up the bag I thought contained Jerry's suit, and hung it in his closet. When he opened the plastic bag the morning of our wedding, there was only a pair of pants—not his—inside. When his parents and I passed Jerry on the road, he was headed to Green Bay and the dry cleaners.

When he arrived there, he slammed the pants on the counter and shouted, "I'm getting married in one hour. Where's my suit?"

The dry cleaners did find the suit. They had simply given me the wrong package. We were married on time at St. Joseph Church in De Pere. We had a small reception in the church basement.

On our way from the church to a family reception at the home of Jerry's former father-in-law, we heard an explosion as we drove over some railroad tracks. Someone had rigged our car with firecrackers. The chief suspect was Jerry's younger brother Bob, another family comedian. A few years later, Jerry and I got a call at 3:00 a.m. On a business trip to Southeast Asia, Bob had been killed when his plane was shot down over Cambodia. His body has never been recovered.

I often wondered if I had been born without a sense of humor. Thanks to Jerry, I discovered that I had humor aplenty after I met and married him.

While I enjoyed Jerry's sense of humor, I became wary of it after he described some of the pranks he played on his first wife. One morning, he told me, he had chased his nude wife out into the hall of their apartment and locked the door behind her. Another time he hid all her bras so that the voluptuous girl had none to wear to her job at St. Norbert College.

I think I fared slightly better, at least when Jerry and I started dating. Shortly after we met, I woke one morning at my home to see an enormous pair of pink bloomers flying from a flagpole on my garage.

Love had returned to my life, bringing with it laughter and fun. My contact with Ken's family lessened with time. Joan faded from the picture. She had divorced her husband, remarried, and was living out of state. I had turned my life around. My hard shell had disintegrated somewhat, and I was no longer so angry with God.

CHAPTER THIRTY THREE

1970s
De Pere
Raising a Big Family

The size of my new family was never an issue for me. I had come from an environment where everything was done in big bunches. Taking on a family with eight children and running a five-bedroom house was no big deal. I ran my household with the precision of a Marine drill sergeant.

In the spring, we set aside a large portion of our backyard for a garden. Jerry and I did the planting. The eight children were assigned the weeding. I made it clear that no weeds were allowed in the garden. Jerry was even more determined. Nicknaming himself "the CEO of Monterey Street," he excelled at supervising the weeders. No playtime till the weeds were gone.

The garden supplied plenty of fresh vegetables: carrots, spinach, lettuce, beans, tomatoes, and broccoli. I remember once when we served broccoli for supper, we insisted all the kids at least try some. Pam, generously graced with her father's sense of humor, asked if she had to also eat the worm that was nestled—cooked, but almost invisible—on one of the flowerets on her plate.

Her question reminds me of something my boss said to me when I worked at CSS (Catholic Social Services). During a Bridge game (we played Bridge during our fifteen-minute morning break), we were discussing the merits of different kinds of apples. I told him how our whole family went apple picking and the kids weren't as fussy as I was when it came to picking the best fruit. I only wanted apples without wormholes. I'm not sure if his reply was entirely serious: "Why would you want an apple that even the worms don't want?"

For produce such as strawberries, peas, and corn, we sought out pick-your-own farms and country orchards. Our mode of travel was in a Volkswagen bus, the most reasonably priced vehicle that could hold all ten of us.

We traveled to nearby farms for most of our produce and to Sturgeon Bay for tart cherries. One year we invited our assistant pastor along for the ride, and did he ever get a whiff of the boisterous, punching and pinching, terribly competitive Seidl family! We had to make our own entertainment; there were no overhead TVs or cell phones or iPods then. We played the alphabet game, the idea being to find each letter of the alphabet, in order, but only on billboards, not passing cars. When that got boring, we brought out the big guns: counting cows.

Back home, as was expected, the whole family went to work. We shucked bushels of corn, canned pecks of peaches and pears, and pitted pails of cherries. Most of the griping came during the pea season. During one pea-shelling session, our sweet little six-year-old Julie—the baby girl of the family—learned a painful lesson: that stuffing peas up her nose was a lot easier than getting them out.

All the hard work paid off with plenty of nutritious food for our big family during the year.

Jerry fancied himself a cook. While I appreciated his help in the kitchen, which was abundant, I was not particularly fond of the old Polish family recipes he had inherited from his mother, such as *pierogi* (sauerkraut or cabbage-filled dumplings), *sultz* (sour jellied pork hocks), and *czernina* (a sour prune and raisin soup). I tried to limit his enthusiasm by refusing to let him grocery shop without me. I cordoned off a portion of the kitchen where his primary duties were peeling vegetables, slicing or cutting up meat and poultry, and serving up kid-approved desserts.

We had a standing edict that the family would eat meals together. To enforce it, we purchased a cowbell that served as our dinner bell—shades of my orphanage days to be sure. Its ring could be heard throughout the neighborhood. When it was time for dinner, whoever was closest to the bell grabbed it and clanged it off our front porch. Jerry said he didn't care whose kids showed up at the dinner table as long as there were eight.

Sewing remained one of my favorite pastimes. I made most of the girls' clothes. For three consecutive years, I entered a "dress-a-doll" contest sponsored by

Kellogg's Citizen's National Bank in Green Bay. The dolls were donated to the Marine Corps' "Toys-for-Tots" program at Christmas.

The first year, 1971, I won the grand prize for my Mary Poppins doll. The two following years I won top prize in category: an Indian princess in the Nationality category in 1972, and "hip chic" in hot pants in the Period Dress category in 1973.

To decorate one of our home's bedrooms, I dug out the bolts of fake fur I had saved from cleaning my husband's basement and made the zebra fabric into a bed spread and pillows shams.

Jerry had a great idea for the tiger fabric. Why not make him a jacket? He liked jackets, owned several, all of them leather, some abounding with fringe. I made him a jacket, nixed the fringe. Jerry liked the finished product so much that he pressured me into making one for myself.

As soon as the second jacket had materialized, Jerry had another idea. "Wouldn't it be cute to dress all the kids in tiger jackets?"

"No way," I said.

Jerry persisted, "Yes, it would."

I stood firm. "No, it wouldn't."

"Yes."

I finally gave in. Chalk one up for Jerry. I made eight more jackets, each with a felt sticker numbered one through eight, from oldest to youngest, sewed to the front. It was another throwback to the orphanage, where our clothes were marked with letters and numbers.

The entire family got into the spirit of the thing, even me. We went everywhere in those jackets. The kids got a kick out of the stares, and even the chuckles, that came our way.

One day, while we were enjoying a visit to the Green Bay Wildlife Sanctuary, wearing the jackets, a woman walked up to us and asked Jerry in dismay if all eight were his children. When he answered yes, she wanted to know if the two youngest, his son Patrick, and my son Paul, were twins

Jerry, ever the jokester replied, "Yes, the boys are twins."

"Oh? How old are they?" the woman inquired.

"Five, but they were born three weeks apart."

The woman did not reply, just looked puzzled as she walked away.

For some reason the rest of the world never caught on to that fad—a whole family cruising around town wearing matching fuzzy tiger jackets.

We vacationed at Waube Lake in Lakewood in northern Wisconsin. Most of the kids became good swimmers. Mary and Lynn were part of a synchronized swimming team one summer. We bought a Pace Arrow motor home and camped in various campsites, including High Cliff State Park on Lake Winnebago near Sherwood, Wisconsin, and Potawatomi State Park northwest of Sturgeon Bay in Door County. In 1975, we traveled to Canada and Florida.

Christmas, as always, was my favorite time of year. The whole family decorated the house and yard, trimmed the trees—we always had more than one—frosted dozens of cookies, shaped popcorn balls, and pulled taffy.

If you think shopping for presents for eight children is a daunting task, try keeping them hidden until Christmas. We employed all the usual hiding places: the attic, the basement, closets, clothes hamper, trash bags, and empty suitcases, most of which were uncovered in minutes. We had to wait until we had grandchildren, and because of the sheer numbers—sixteen—we gave them cash.

We out-sleuthed the grandkids every year. Once it was felt teddy bear ornaments with buttoned back flaps to hide the money, and we scattered them throughout one of several Christmas trees. Another year it was cash rolled up in colored paper and inserted it into clear glass ornaments. Naturally, once the first one was found—after several hours—the gig was up. Other years we put the money in envelopes and slid the envelopes under oriental rugs, or taped them to the back of pictures hanging on the wall. The one they finally had to give up on was when we hid the envelopes in grandpa's jacket pocket. All's fair.

Christmas morning at the Seidl residence could only be described as "organized chaos." Jerry and I had decreed that no one was allowed downstairs until we got up. That decree did not stop the eight from rising at 4:00 a.m. and tapping on the master bedroom door. We'd manage to hold them off till about 5:00 a.m.

When we were all together in the family room, presents were distributed, wrapping paper ripped off to screams of delight, and the search for missing batteries began. Then it was off to church and visits with relatives.

Before long we were overflowing with teens and their activities. We could have had our own cheerleading squad with Barb, Lynn, Pam and Julie. Kathy went out for basketball, Patrick for football, Paul for football and track. Lynn played the trumpet and french horn in the band. She was also in the chorus. Barb played the guitar (taught by her dad), oboe and sax. She was also in french club, and in 1973 earned her own money for a trip to Paris. Kathy was the skater in the family, eventually going on to compete in roller skating dance competition. Mary was in art class and won Best in State one year. Patrick, my gentle giant, spent a good deal of time in his dad's workshop, learning things that would help him start his own successful business one day.

Being part of the Seidl clan was being part of fun, jokes, music, and sibling rivalry. One summer the family hosted a huge water fight. It started in the front yard when someone poured water "accidentally" on someone else's head. Immediate retribution was called for. Soon the whole neighborhood, the eight Seidl kids, and Max, our German Shepherd, were in on the action.

Over the years, at family gatherings the kids confessed to pranks they played on each other and some of the stuff they did that we never knew about, things that would have gotten them grounded for life. Like the tree outside an upstairs bedroom they climbed down at night. They have yet to tell us what they did after that.

One of the kids gave me a card one year that I hung on my bulletin board at work. I still have it. Under a picture of Garfield the Cat is a caption that reads: "You can't scare me. I have children."

In 1976, Jerry and I decided to move to the country for the space and the fresh air. We chose to build an English Tudor-style home in Greenleaf, a community south of De Pere.

The house was primarily a do-it-yourself project. Our two oldest, Barb and Kathy, had moved into their own apartments. The six kids, ages ten to sixteen, still at home, helped build the house from the basement up. We had sold the house in De Pere before we could finish the new one, so we temporarily lived in our motor home. I seem to remember all of us living in cramped quarters once before.

Some of the work required professionals, so often there were workmen on site. Keeping Max in tow during those times turned out to be a challenge. While this big, black-and-tan bundle of German Shepherd was a complete pussycat with us, he was also very protective. We had to keep him in the motor home or tied up in the garage. However, Max needed to burn off his excessive energy, so I'd take him out for daily runs. I was on my way back from a run one day when I spotted one of the workers out in the front yard. So did Max. He went into overdrive.

"I hope you got a tight rein on that dog!" the worker shouted. There was no effective place for him to run or to hide.

Too bad *Candid Camera* wasn't there. Max took off. I hung onto the leash as tight as I could; ended up sprawled flat on the ground in the mud, with Max dragging me across the yard. But I never let go of that leash.

Max once lost a battle with a skunk. That little episode cost him many tomato juice baths and a month's confinement in the garage.

While I loved the idea of living in the country, all was not perfect. Too late, Jerry and I realized that serving as our own general contractors was a big mistake. We had gotten some bad advice and misinformation, the worst being the cost of heating the house with electric heat. The estimate from Wisconsin Public Service was way off. Also, cleaning up the only water supply, a man-made pond in the middle of the development, cost a fortune.

The children went to separate schools a distance from the house, a grade school and high school. Coordinating activities between the schools wasn't easy. The kids who wanted after-school jobs had no transportation back and forth except bikes, and we didn't allow that.

What I regret more than anything about that venture is that we never gave the children a say in the matter. We didn't ask them how they felt about moving away from their friends.

We sold the house after living in it for just one year.

PART THREE

Forgiveness is choosing to love. It is the first skill of self-giving love.

—Mohandas K. Gandhi, 1869–1948

CHAPTER THIRTY FOUR

1979
Green Bay
A Calling

W^e were now living in Green Bay, having purchased a home on Hazelwood Lane. With six kids still living at home with us, we needed a four-bedroom house and had a dickens of a time finding one. After our fiasco in the country, we were a little sour about building again.

One of the things I had not taken into account when signing on with Jerry was that it takes a fair amount of dollars to raise eight children; maybe two can live as cheaply as one, but not ten. Two years after Jerry and I were married, in 1971, I decided to get a paying job. Office work was all I knew, but my secretarial skills were rusty. I had not held a job (I say that with a smile on my face) since I was pregnant with Kathy; that was in 1957.

When I contacted an employment agency, the agent I talked to said she didn't have any office openings for someone with my current lack of expertise (she was kinder than that) but that I could make good money as a waitress, and there was an opening at Bilotti's, an up-scale restaurant and Packer hang-out on Green Bay's west side. Although I had no experience waitressing, I was hired to work evenings and weekends. I took the job because I could be home mornings and after school with my children.

After eight years waitressing, I knew I had to do something far more fulfilling. It was time to brush up on my clerical skills. I signed up for accounting courses and computer courses at Northeast Wisconsin Technology College (NWTC) in Green Bay.

At the same time, I put my name in at an employment agency, and one day about a year later, I got a call. There was an opening for a secretary/case-aide in the Catholic Social Services office (formerly The Apostolate). For a moment, I was thrown off-guard. In that split second, a slice of my early life passed before my eyes: being dropped off at the orphanage; not being told where my sister was; my removal from a foster home to Good Shepherd's Home. I couldn't say all this to the agent on the other end of the line. She was telling me what a great opportunity this could be for me.

"Hi, you still there?" she asked when I didn't answer right away. "Are you interested?"

I knew I couldn't keep her on the phone forever while my subconscious meandered through fields of resentment. Not wanting to seem ungrateful for the research she had done, I answered in the most confident voice I could muster. "Sure."

"Okay. I'll call you with the details."

I don't remember everything that went through my mind after I hung up the phone. The agent had said that this job could be a good starting place for me. The experience would make it easier to move up to another job because employers preferred to hire persons who were currently working in positions similar to what they were looking for.

After searching my soul for a reason to say no, I set my misgivings aside. It couldn't hurt to take a look. After all, the orphanage days, and all that went with them, *were* long gone, and I wouldn't have to accept the job. I could tell the agent that I preferred to concentrate on my studies. Besides, I wouldn't have to stay if I didn't like it.

About a half hour later, the agent called back. "Bea, it's all set. Your appointment is at eleven o'clock on Saturday at the office on Madison Street with Mary Anne Patterson, the office manager. Take the stairs to the lower level."

"OK," I said, trying to keep my voice pleasant. I wasn't about to alienate the person who was going to find me my next job.

I faced the job interview that Saturday morning in 1979 with more confidence than I felt. I was of two minds. The possibility of working for the agency that placed me at the orphanage intrigued me. *What kind of people might I be working with? Where might this job lead?*

On the other hand, I was more scared than I wanted to admit. Catholic Social Services, or at least its counterpart, represented the pain and loneliness I had known as a child, the pain I hadn't dealt with.

As I entered the building, I noted the quiet, somber atmosphere. Memories of other, darker places flooded my mind. I didn't want to be there. *Forget the whole thing. You can't handle this.* However, I knew it would be unprofessional not to keep the appointment I had made, and it certainly wouldn't do much to enhance any future job prospects, so I continued down the stairs.

But I had already made my decision. I said the words almost out loud. "There's no way in hell I'm going to work here."

After the interview, which included typing and English tests, I went home to consider what had just happened. I thought I had a good chance of getting the job, and wasn't that, after all, my goal? To get away from waitressing and into an office job? I thought again about the long, lonely, harsh years at the orphanage. I couldn't put to rest the fact that I thought the caseworkers back then had done me an injustice by deciding that the best place for me was the orphanage, and leaving me there for eight years. Would taking a job with the organization change any of that?

I challenged myself to come up with some positives about St. Joe's and thought immediately of Sister Amanda. Sister Muriel and the choir also came to mind, as did Father John and some of my teachers. They had instilled in me a strong sense of right and wrong, provided a high-standard education, and endued their peerless work ethic.

I answered the call for a second interview with the Social Services director. His concern before he offered me the job was whether I could make the transition from working nights as a waitress to working days in an office. It took me only a second to answer. "If I don't get this job," I predicted, "within a year, I will be working in someone's office." I got the job. That was in February of 1979.

At the time, Catholic Social Services, part of Catholic Charities, was on South Madison Street in Green Bay. The offices were in a building (now Cathedral Book & Gift) next door to the rectory of St. Francis Xavier Cathedral. Some of the other offices in the building were Education, Social Concerns, Missions, and Retreat House, although some of them changed names over the years.

From the very first, I felt like I was part of a big family. The work wasn't all that exciting, but the people were warm and friendly. We celebrated birthdays, weddings, and babies. One of the girls that I worked with went on to work in the Bishop's Charities office. By the time I retired we were both working in the Computer Services office. I had attended her wedding, congratulated her when her two babies were born, and relished their college days right along with her.

The office was close to the downtown area so some of us used our noon hours for shopping, or we'd go to the old Kaaps restaurant on North Washington Street for lunch or some of their chocolates. At Christmastime, we'd catch the mechanical displays in Prange's windows.

No one knew about my time at the orphanage; I hadn't as yet shared any of that information. I thought if anyone knew I had been in an orphanage it would diminish me in their eyes, and I didn't want anything to change. I was getting comfortable in my position, mingling with nuns and priests on a daily basis.

After three years of this seemingly idyllic situation, things changed again.

In the early 1950s, a new Chapel and Bona Hall had been built on the orphanage grounds (the orphanage was demolished in 1981). By 1982, there was a plan in place to relocate Catholic Social Services and other diocesan offices to Bona Hall.

I was highly apprehensive about the move. I had left the orphanage in 1950, vowing never to go back. With the scheduled date for the move fast approaching, I considered quitting my job and finding another. Anyway, my current duties—mimeographing, answering the telephone, and doing intake interviews—were not what I wanted to do for the rest of my life.

On the other hand, I had begun to develop new feelings toward Catholic Social Services, its programs and staff, their sensitivity and dedication. But it was more than that. I believed I was part of something important, that it was an honor to work for the Catholic Diocese of Green Bay.

I thought back to the day my caseworker, Ellen, drove me to the orphanage. My mother had told me not to talk to her, so I didn't. After Ellen dropped me off, I was too frightened to think about her. But when she didn't come back, I thought she didn't care what happened to me. I remembered an incident when I was at my second foster home. My caseworker picked me up in her car one afternoon and took me out for hamburgers. She was very nice, tried to get me to open up. I wouldn't talk to her, didn't answer her questions. I didn't give her a chance, only attitude: *Why does she have to keep checking up on me? Can't she just leave me alone?* That's how I viewed all caseworkers. They had a job to do, and I was a number in their caseload.

The decision to stay at the diocese helped me reform a lot of my thinking. I would have to consider it one of the smartest moves I ever made: not to move.

Now all I had to do was show up at my ill-remembered stomping grounds every day.

CHAPTER THIRTY FIVE

1982
Bona Hall
Back to the Beginning

More than thirty years had gone by since I'd last been here. The bitterness and resentment that I had built over the years lingered. Still buried was everything I didn't want to remember.

It was a cold January day. I was coming from the west side of Green Bay, so I took the Riverside Drive entrance, arriving early to be by myself for a few minutes. As I drove toward Bona Hall and my new office, I remembered my first impressions from 1942: the huge building, thinking it had to be a castle; the tower with the shiny cross; the big rounded windows; a tall wooden door closing out the light, enveloping me in darkness, separating me from my family and the world outside.

St Joseph's Orphanage was gone. Still hanging in there were the apple trees, gnarled and barren in the dead of winter. As I passed alongside Bona Hall into what was now a parking lot, the montage ahead played like a silent movie, each scene conjuring up its own memories: the Bungalow, harsh and stormy; Melania Hall, hot and steamy; Bosco Hall, a dark closet, a brother and sister lost and alone. Happier scenes too: swings and a slide; snow and toboggans, and laughing children.

After parking my car, I strolled around the grounds for a short time ending up by a sidewalk leading to Bona Hall. I walked past the chapel and the statues of the children and Our Lady of Fatima, up the steps, and through the glass door of the entrance. I had never been inside Bona Hall. It was built after I left the orphanage. Carol Rosik (now Kramer), the other case-aide who had been hired the same day as me, and Mary Anne Patterson, the office manager were already there. Mary Anne showed us where our offices would be, after which she gave us a tour of the building. I tried to visualize kids sleeping or playing in the rooms that had been transformed into offices. The rooms were smaller with a lot more light than I remembered in the old building.

As case-aides, Carol and I attended seminars with the social workers, thereby getting to know them personally as well as professionally. I found them to be warm, dedicated, and compassionate people. My supervisor (a social worker) was a no-nonsense type who stopped me in my tracks the minute I went to the negative about anything. She is one of the most considerate and sensitive people I know.

Another social worker, George Arens, was one of the many wonderful people that I was lucky enough to get to know during my years at Catholic Social Services. He had a ready laugh and good sense of humor. I'm sharing his story because not only is it fascinating and very special, but also because he was the director of casework services at the orphanage during the 1960s.

On the recommendation of a Capuchin priest, on April 1, 1946, Father Edward J. Flanagan of Boys Town in Omaha, Nebraska, hired George as a counselor.
        George was the head counselor for the Boys Town choir—which numbered forty-two boys—when the group went on its first national tour in November 1946. The choir performed at all the major concert venues, including Carnegie Hall. The concerts sold out wherever they went. They crossed the country by bus. On one of their stops coming out of New York, they came across another bus making a tour: the Von Trappe family singers (*The Sound of Music*). Some of the kids exchanged buses for a short while until it was time to part company for their respective tours.

George accepted the job as psychiatric social worker at St. Joseph's Orphanage in 1960. Now called St. Joseph's Home for Children, the focus had changed to residential treatment. Bona Hall became the children's residence, the main building used mainly for the classrooms.
        Before the Cuban Missile Crisis hit in 1962, the head of the American Refugee program asked the director at the orphanage if he could take some

of the Cuban children who were being sent to America by their parents. A special emergency program was established in 1961 to accept Cuban children at the orphanage. Thirty-eight Cuban children were cared for between 1961 and 1964.

While transporting some of the children from the airport to St. Joe's, George was trying to get across to them that they were in Green Bay but wasn't having much luck until they passed City Stadium. When he mentioned the Packers, the children knew where they were. They remembered the televised games they had seen.

The girls' program at the orphanage was discontinued in 1967, and until 1977, St. Joseph's Home for Children accepted only boys ages eight to sixteen with special needs that required professional care and treatment. After all the programs at St. Joseph's were discontinued, George became a counselor for Catholic Social Services.

I found it impossible to be sad or down in George's presence. He is the most up-beat man I ever met, and a man who is very proud of his family.

During my early years at the diocese, there was not a lot of employee turnover. Over time, walls and doors were moved or added, offices and departments changed, lay people hired to replace some of the nuns and priests. What remained steady was the ever-friendly, helpful staff. I was privileged to cross paths with five bishops during my years at the diocese.

Besides daily mass at the chapel on the grounds, the diocese afforded its employees many opportunities for interaction with each other. A picnic in the summer provided fun and games for the whole family. The highlight of the day was the baseball game with the team captains vying to see who would get Bishop Banks on their team.

We went on yearly retreats, many of them at Camp Tekawitha on Loon Lake in Shawano County. One year the retreat was at St. Norbert Abbey. We were all in the chapel and it was such a beautiful spring day that the doors were left open. Early in the service, we had unexpected visitors. Oblivious of the seriousness of the goings-on, a mama duck, followed by her numerous yellow babies, waddled down the center aisle, stealing the show and bringing on a plentitude of smiles. Just another day at the office.

An annual Christmas party included a live band for dancing. Each year one department hosted the evening's entertainment, which always included riotous skits.

In 1984, I went back to school. The kids were all out of the house by now and I needed a new direction. I took computer courses and programming courses while continuing to work full time.

When a bookkeeping position opened in the diocesan finance department at the Chancery (the administrative office of the diocese), I applied for it and was hired.

That department was located in the four-story, red brick building, formerly the bishop's home, on Webster Avenue. Bishop Stanislaus V. Bona had lived and worked there until 1968 when Bishop Wycislo was installed as the bishop of Green Bay. In 1976, Bishop Wycislo built a ranch home—to be the bishop's home—on the grounds between the Chancery and Bosco Hall.

Looking east toward Bosco Hall, 1941
Courtesy of the Neville Public Museum of Brown County

Unlike the other buildings on the grounds, I had never seen the inside of the Chancery. In 1950 when I graduated from eighth grade, my classmates and I had assembled on the back steps of the building to have our commencement picture taken with Bishop Bona (girls were not allowed in the building). Now, after all these years, I would be working there.

The Chancery (razed in 2010) housed the development office as well as the Tribunal and the Archives. The finance office, which included computer services at the time, was on the first floor.

What I remember about the Chancery building was the beautiful woodwork. There was a small elevator in the building, but I took the stairs when going from one floor to another; I get claustrophobic in elevators. The artwork displayed in some of the rooms was from the days when the bishops lived there. One that was particularly moving depicted Our Lord's Last Supper with his twelve apostles. It hung in the break room (a former dining room) where staff would gather to share birthdays and family stories. Again, it was the people that I met and worked with in the Chancery, the priests, nuns, and lay people that brought me a sense of worth that seemed lacking in other areas of my life.

Chancery, upper right; Bona Hall, bottom, 1967
Courtesy of the Neville Public Museum of Brown County

The diocese had acquired a new computer system prior to Bishop Adam Maida's installation as Bishop of the Green Bay Diocese. At the time, I was doing the most basic bookkeeping. The computer supervisor moved into a different position and my boss offered me the job supervising the computer system. Though I had no experience, I realized I had just been handed a great opportunity and was determined to make my boss proud and prove to him that I could do it. I spent many late nights in the computer department studying and working until the night cleaning crews had to lock up. Then I took the books home and stayed up until the wee hours continuing my studies there. The diocese provided plenty of training, some locally, and some in Milwaukee and Chicago.

When the diocese moved to a PC-based system, I found myself back at square one. Combining my previous training and programming courses, I took on the new system's database program. Many of the diocesan departments were compiling information manually, so I wrote and documented database applications for them, trained the users and taught them how to use the applications. I worked with almost every department, and much of the staff in the diocesan offices, and in the process, wrote over thirty databases, supported, and maintained them.

Along with the social workers and office staff, I had gotten to know many of the priests and nuns who worked in the diocesan offices. I worked with two nuns while creating a database for Silver Lake College in Manitowoc. One of the nuns and I were part of a mutual admiration society. While I admired her as an educator and servant of God, she admired me for my ability to make her database do whatever she wanted it to do. While Computer Services was evolving, I had four different bosses: a monsignor, a nun, the finance officer, and the director of communications.

When the diocese moved its offices to Bona Hall, I knew there would be daily reminders of my days at the orphanage. The Bungalow, Melania Hall, Bosco Hall, and the grounds surrounding the compound revived dozens of memories. A small bridge spanned the ravine behind Melania Hall. Once leading to the farm buildings, it now led to a walking trail, a great place for quiet, noontime reflection. The tunnels that once ran from the main building to Melania and to Bosco were closed up, but there were two new tunnels, one from Melania to Bosco, and one from Bona Hall to the chapel. The tunnels, used as a means of getting from one building to another during inclement weather, were also considered fallout shelters.

The bungalow, former home of the orphanage director, had quite a negative impact on me as a child. Bishop Wycislo, bishop emeritus, was living there now. I was working in Computer Services, and from time to time, he asked for help with a computer problem he was having. Walking into that house for the first time in over forty years helped ease some crippling memories. Bishop made it a peaceful, warm, and welcoming home. It was not the building I remembered where an angry nun and belligerent child had come to grips with their clashing personalities. I was awed by this humble and holy man, a man dedicated to his priesthood. He was a man of love, for the Church and for people. He shared his talents and himself with the world. I loved working with him.

For many years, shame prevented me from telling anyone that I had been in the orphanage. When I finally did—I don't remember when that was—I was uncomfortable with their questions. I had not yet reconciled myself to much of my past. Before I retired, I told some of my co-workers that for years I had been trying to write a book about my experience.

In 1994, when I read an article about bringing orphanages back as a way to care for abandoned and neglected children, I started thinking seriously about my childhood and the Apostolate. While being raised in an orphanage was not, by a longshot, ideal, I wondered if the caseworker had gotten me out of a worse situation. I don't know what would have happened had I not been taken away from my parents. Either way, I did not have a happy childhood. Maybe it was time to finish the story.

For now though, life was good. I was blessed with a big family, friends, a job that I loved, and stellar co-workers. I had a nice home with beautiful gardens, two cats, and an ever-increasing number of grandchildren.

I needed to bring God back into my life.

CHAPTER THIRTY SIX

1991
Finding God

I knew that at some point in my life I would have to confront and deal
with the bitterness of my childhood, adolescence, and the aftermath of
my first husband's death. High on my list of priorities was restoring my
relationship with God.

During my years at St. Joe's, the nuns and priests attempted to instill in
me a belief in him and a trust in his will. I thought God should be someone
I could see and hear, not some mystical being floating around up in the sky
somewhere. At the tender age of eight, when I made my first communion,
hell, damnation, and the devil seemed real enough. Not so much a benevolent
God.

Looking back, though I grumbled at what seemed like tedious and
repetitious church services, I can say that inwardly I loved the Catholic practices
that brought me peace: the celebration of the Mass, Holy Communion, and
many of the prayers. Especially the Angelus, a devotion in memory of the
Incarnation (the doctrine that the son of God was conceived in the womb of
Mary). The ringing of the Angelus bell every morning, noon, and evening
was a call to prayer, and everyone stopped what they were doing to say the
Angelus. I especially loved if I happened to be outside on a bright sunny day
when the bell tolled. It was like Heaven opened up and I could speak directly
to the Blessed Virgin Mary.

But after the loss of my first love, Ken, I threw away these practices. And
I gave up on God. I maintained the core values I had been raised on, but I
counted on no one but myself.

In 1991, at first unaware of what was happening to me, I began my journey back to God. What was leading me? Surprisingly, it was my love of sewing.

In my youth, I had taken up embroidery, selecting old-fashioned stamped pieces with flowers and alphabets. When counted cross-stitch became the craze, I took that up as well. Designs in this form of needlework were stitched from charts over squares of threads counted out on unmarked fabric. They were often packaged in kits.

One kit that I purchased portrayed a deer surrounded by flowers, and a butterfly. There was a proverb above the deer which I basically ignored. When the piece was completed, the saying's absence left a bare spot, so I filled in the required thirty-six letters, had the piece framed, and hung it in my bedroom.

The picture hung on the wall in my bedroom in such a way that I couldn't miss it when I walked into the room. The words were just about eye level and they started to "stick" in my memory. Then one day I was able to put meaning to the proverb. It read: To See Creation is to Know There is a Creator.

God had just reintroduced himself. I could see what I had missed all along. God isn't just sitting on high ordering the Ten Commandments, judging, and punishing us. He gives us a whole, wide, wonderful world to enjoy. The moon and the stars, gorgeous sunsets, colorful rainbows. He makes roses burst into bloom, scattering their heavenly scents. He gives us beautiful birds and animals. And he gives us precious babies that smile and coo.

This time when God reached out to me, I didn't push him away.

But God was not finished with me yet. In 1998, when Jerry was sixty-six years old, he was diagnosed with Parkinson's disease (a neurological disorder) and dementia. It was a blow for the whole family. Jerry first talked about how he lost his sense of smell. I noticed how his walk changed. For a man who was normally very graceful, his walk started to resemble more of a shuffle. His posture became stooped. He lost a lot of weight. He was no longer the out-going person he had been.

For more than a year and a half before Jerry died, he went to the Aging Resource Center during the day while I worked full time at the diocese. A gal that I played bridge with had gone through the same experience with her husband, only she had decided to retire from her job to stay at home with him. She told me, "Whatever you do, don't quit your job. Find a way to keep working. It will keep you sane."

The diocese came through for me again, granting me the time I needed to transport Jerry to and from the Center, and to his doctor appointments. My co-workers supported me with their prayers and good wishes during some tough days.

We kept Jerry at home for as long as we could. Eventually, Unity Hospice in Green Bay helped with his care. Three weeks before he died, when we could no longer handle him, we put him in a nursing home. He died March 4, 2007.

Before he died, Barb, Jerry's oldest daughter, approached me to see if I could arrange to have Jerry buried in the Catholic Church, though he had not been a practicing Catholic for a number of years. She said it would mean a lot to the kids. I had resumed my Catholicism but mostly stayed in the background, hypocrite that I was. Our wonderful pastor, Bishop Robert Morneau, allowed Jerry to be buried from Resurrection Parish in Green Bay.

The picture with the deer hangs above my computer today and will remain so. Every time I look at it, I'm reminded once more how God is a presence in this world of ours.

CHAPTER THIRTY SEVEN

2009
Loving and Forgiving

Learning to forgive is the hardest for me. For too many years, I lived with hatred that carried over into my private life. I hated the people I thought had wronged me. I viewed them as I viewed most things those days, shortsightedly. I kept my family and friends at arm's length, afraid of getting hurt. And once hurt, I didn't give people a chance to hurt me again.

I had to learn that it wasn't people or an organization that had wronged me, but an idea I had planted in my head. My years at the diocese proved to be a path to understanding. I believe those years gave me the insight I needed to find the ability to forgive. It took me many years to realize I might have been worse off had I been left in my home with my mother and father. The attitudes of the priests, nuns, and social workers I worked with at the diocese helped me realize that the caseworkers were doing a tough job with limited resources.

"What Is This Thing Called Love?" Cole Porter asked in his 1929 song. I had to find out for myself. The sisters at St. Joseph's Orphanage weren't equipped to give us the love we craved. A few tried, but most had no training in childcare. Nuns like Sister Edythe had no patience with the children.

Other than my sister, I don't recall love in my home. My mother was there, but I don't remember feeling any love. Maybe she was too busy with a new baby every year, or maybe she herself had none to draw from. I barely remember my younger sister and three brothers. I think I was in my own little fantasy world. I don't remember my father at all. I see fathers—usually in church because I take the time to look around—holding their babies with such tenderness I want to cry. How envious I am. I see young families holding their children close. How envious I am.

I was witness to an act of pure love on a flight home from Florida in 2009. I had just buckled myself into the aisle seat in the last row and was settling down to finish reading the last few chapters of Bill O'Reilly's *A Bold Fresh Piece of Humanity* when a young woman with a baby asked to be let in. I admit to being irritated by the situation. Not only did I have to get unbuckled and get out of my seat, but I also figured I would not be able to read my book because there would be a screaming baby next to me.

I could not have been more wrong. The mother settled the baby in the window seat and she sat in the middle seat. She then proceeded to spend the entire flight softly talking and singing to her seventeen-month-old son. She played word games with him. She asked him which lullaby he wanted her to sing, and then sang it. She gently massaged/tickled his arms, legs, and little bare toes. "Ears and elbows, knees and toes," she sang as she pointed to each. He was able to repeat everything she said. When the plane was at the higher altitudes, the mother cradled the baby's head while she constantly reassured him. The minute he started fussing, she tried a new tact to calm him.

I asked the woman if I could use her name and her son's name in a book I was writing. She agreed and we exchanged pleasantries as we disembarked.

Thank you, Amy. And Magnus, you are a lucky boy.

I did finish your book, Bill O'Reilly, and I loved it, but you were trumped on that trip.

Witnessing that scene made me think about all the love I had missed because of my stubbornness. Could it be that I wasn't paying attention? Maybe I didn't recognize love, being so involved in self-pity as I was. I had a cock-eyed view of love. How could strangers love me when my own mother and father didn't? I thought I had to give my friends permission to love me, and I couldn't do that because I didn't think I was deserving.

FINAL THOUGHTS:

I've learned that it is possible to love, even though I knew almost none as a child. I know my sister loved me.

I certainly found love with Ken, my first husband. I'm sure I was never able to fully appreciate that wonderful human being. Oh, if I could have him back for a day, what I would tell him. How much I love him, his boyish charm. How sorry I am for putting him off, like when he'd come home from work and put his arms around me, and I'd brush him off; too busy—cleaning something.

And with Jerry, my clown, who helped me conquer my shyness and helped me discover I could be an extrovert, who showed me I had a sense of humor and who taught me to laugh. I loved that, wherever we were, he held my hand.

Some of my friends have shown me love, but I sloughed it off. I just thought they were nice people who did nice things. I didn't know what I didn't know.

Deep in my heart, I love my big family. With the grandkids getting married and having their own kids, it keeps growing.

I've learned that I need to forgive. Because I chose to be unforgiving, I cut myself off from my family. It was a price I was willing to pay, but my children paid as well. They were deprived of a family that may have helped shaped who they would become. We'll never know.

Unforgiveness hurts more than the person who refuses to forgive. My father means nothing to me, but maybe it's time to forgive my mother. I chose not to know her, but if she were alive today, I would want to hear her story.

The shell is almost gone now; only a few rough edges remain.

I've closed a lot of doors in my life, but I believe I have opened many more.

EPILOGUE

My sister and I have a close friendship today. Finding out that she was my half-sister is a hurt that I have kept in my heart. I guess I've never really resolved that issue. I understand now that she cannot be the mother I had searched for my whole life.

Glenda tried to keep in contact with me through relatives, but I wanted nothing to do with her. She left me at the orphanage, and after I was out on my own taking care of myself, she wanted me to embrace her as my mother. I didn't feel anything for her. For me, the word "mother" was just that, a word.

As for my brothers and younger sister, I didn't know them. As far as I was concerned, I had no family. I recall Glenda visiting me in 1955 accompanied by my four younger siblings. She must have picked them up from their foster homes that day. After a few awkward hours—I have no recollection of what we did—we parted company. I made no effort to contact any of them after that.

Glenda phoned me after she heard of Ken's death. She told me how sorry she was. I told her that he was the best thing that had ever happened to me. I listened to her for a minute or two. Then, not wanting to let her hear me cry, I hung up. She was working as a cook at a mental health hospital in Chicago when she died in 1982.

There was a mystery surrounding Joan and our Uncle Matthew, Glenda's brother-in-law, married to her sister Alice. Matthew treated Joan like a daughter and promised she would always be taken care of.

When Lawrence (Aunt Alice and Uncle Matthew's son) visited his Aunt Glenda in Chicago in 1981, she joked about Joan's origins. He guessed at what she meant, but kept his thoughts to himself.

Uncle Matthew made a deathbed confession to Lawrence that he had fathered Joan. This information was not disclosed for a while, but eventually started to come out as the "cousins" reunited in the '90s. Matthew's sisters started to guess and one of them told Joan of her suspicions at their second reunion. Joan confronted Lawrence, and he confirmed to her that it was true.

Joan and I had grown apart around the time of Ken's death and afterward. She had nine children with her first husband and later divorced him. After re-marrying in 1980, she and her family moved out of state. I was busy with my own family of eight.

On a trip to Florida in 2009, I was reunited with my younger sister Ann, whom I hadn't seen for more than fifty years. My niece, Joan's daughter, found Ann with the help of her Uncle Lawrence.

When my niece learned I was writing this story, she thought I might want to talk to Ann. We arranged to meet near Ann's home, also in Florida. I was disappointed that Ann hardly spoke. She would not, or could not, share anything about the orphanage. I asked her about her foster home. She replied, "Oh, it wasn't so bad." I had heard differently from a woman who had been at the same foster home as Ann with two of my brothers. That's a horror story all its own. Most of the information I got that day was from Ann's daughter.

In 1953, Joe and Ann were sent to a foster home on a farm in Wisconsin. Frank went to the same foster home in 1957. After suffering unspeakable cruelties at the farm, the three went to live with Glenda in Chicago in the early 1960s. Ann married, had three children, then divorced.

Ann's daughter dropped out of high school when she was a sophomore and went to work as a waitress to support her mother. She earned her GED while working full time. Eventually, she bought a home in Florida. Today she is married to a police officer and the mother of two children. Ann lived with her daughter for a short time. She now resides in a small retirement community.

My brother Joe worked as a janitor at a school in Chicago until his death a few years ago. Frank ended up a male prostitute somewhere in Chicago. My brother Edward, born developmentally disabled, went to a Chippewa Falls institution for the mentally handicapped in Wisconsin in 1952. He reportedly died in a drowning accident in August of 1972.

POSTSCRIPT

1942 – 1957
Brothers and Sisters
A Story to be Told

In 1942, when I went to St. Joseph's Orphanage and Joan to Good Shepherd's, four-year-old Joe and three-year-old Ann were put in the nursery at St. Joe's. Twenty-month-old Frank and three-week-old Edward were placed together in a foster home. From time to time, the two boys were shuffled between that foster home and the orphanage, reportedly when the family took vacations.

In 1953, Joe and Ann, fifteen and fourteen respectively, were sent to a foster home on a farm in Wisconsin. Frank went to the same foster home in 1957 when he was seventeen. Not all children leaving the orphanage attended high school; some became farm workers, others house workers.

Around that time, a girl by the name of Evelyn was sent to the same farm. She had been at the orphanage after I left. In 2008, through my niece, I met Evelyn, and she's the one who related the following story to me.

At the farm, Evelyn, Joe, and Ann became close friends. Ann was an extremely shy child, Joe a soft-spoken, unobtrusive child, Evelyn more outgoing. Evelyn treated Joe as though he were a brother, and did so right up until his death.

Over the years, that foster home housed over twenty children. The couple who owned the farm, let's call them Lewis and Marge, had no children of their own.

Evelyn and Ann both lived in fear of Lewis, but Evelyn knew he was singling her out. He would make her strip down to her underwear and walk around the room while he'd strike her with a switch. In the evening after supper, she had to rub Lewis's back, scratch his head, and occasionally shampoo his hair (with Breck shampoo). Incidentally, the kids didn't get to eat the same food as Lewis and Marge. Lewis ridiculed the kids, calling them "stupid asses," "stupid cows," and "pigs." He called Evelyn a "squaw," but he beat her only once.

It was the last Christmas that the three kids were there together. Marge had trimmed the tree and wrapped the presents—pajamas for each of them—and put them under the tree. A drunken Lewis came into the room, tore down the Christmas tree, ripped the trimmings off the tree, smashed the balls, and cut up all the presents. Evelyn was so angry that she put her face right up to his and said, "Why didn't you smash the Breck too?"

After the beating, she told him if he ever beat her again, she would kill him. She begged to be taken back to the orphanage, to no avail.

Ann had poor eyesight and wore glasses. Lewis taunted and belittled her. He beat her one time with a belt buckle. Evelyn and Joe could hear her cries but were powerless to stop it.

The foster children did most of the farm work. Joe would be harnessed to the tractor, with the tongue between his legs. Ann and Evelyn had to push the tractor. If Joe were to slip and let go, they could have been crushed.

They scavenged an old *Monopoly* game and played every evening, evoking more of Lewis's ire. "You like to play so much; okay, play." As a new punishment, he made them stay up all night playing the game.

When Frank came to the farm, he also had ideas about Evelyn. He and Joe got into many scuffles over this, but as Evelyn's friend and protector, Joe was able to hold Frank at bay. Lewis was something else. He wouldn't tolerate any of it.

To punish Frank, Lewis tied the boy's hands behind his back, but Lewis couldn't hang on to him and Frank made a run for it. Lewis chased Frank in his car trying to run him down. After Frank was caught, he was brutally beaten. Some of Frank's beatings were with a two-by-four, or Lewis would bang his head on the kitchen table until his hair came out in the front of his head.

Evelyn told me that one time she saw Joe, naked, hanging by his hands from the rafters in the barn while Lewis beat him.

When the Apostolate staff made visits and asked the kids how things were, they said "fine." They knew if they said anything else, they would be beaten. Somehow the caseworker didn't catch on, that something was amiss.

Evelyn shared other stories with me, too numerous to mention here. In spite of the cruelty, some of the kids, including Joe and Ann, stayed on after the age of eighteen when they could have left. They didn't know anything else, didn't expect anything else.

Demolition, March, 1981
Courtesy of the Diocese of Green Bay Archives

ACKNOWLEDGEMENTS

Thanks to all without whose invaluable help, I would not have been able to put these stories together.

My sister Joan for sharing some really tough stories that, for years, I knew nothing about, and for all her hugs.

Joan's daughter, for her tremendous help in putting the family history together.

My younger sister's daughter for shedding light on her mom's life.

All my former "co-inmates" who helped stir up so many orphanage memories, the good, the bad, and the funny.

George Arens, for his vintage orphanage stories.

John and Olivia in the Diocesan Archives, for pictures and history.

Neville Public Museum for pictures.

Margaret Rawlings for the *Press Gazette* article.

Pat Kasten for reviewing the book and for her publishing advice.

Betsy Foley for her encouragement.

And finally, my deep thanks to Joanne Flemming, my editor, for her friendship, good advice, and for keeping me on the right path.

BIBLIOGRAPHY

Bay Beach Amusement Park. Green Bay, Wisconsin: City of Green Bay Archives.

Catholic Diocese of Green Bay Archives. History of St. Joseph's Home, Green Bay, Wisconsin.

Collum, Maggie (Margaret Rawlings). "Landmark Going." Editorial in *Green Bay Press Gazette*. Green Bay, Wisconsin, January 6, 1981.

The Green Bay Diocese Apostolate. Catholic Social Service Bureau. "A Little History. The Historical Development of the Green Bay Apostolate." *Catholic Charities Newsletter, Volume I, No. 3*. October 1966.

Leman, Dr. Kevin and Randy Carlson. *Unlocking the Secrets of Your Childhood Memories*. Nashville, Tennessee: Thomas Nelson Publishers. 1989.

McDowell, M. Evaluation of St. Joseph's Orphan Asylum. Green Bay, Wisconsin. 1940.

One Hundred Years of Service of St. Joseph Home for Children in the Green Bay Diocese 1877–1977. October 23, 1977

"The orphanage: is it time to bring it back? – Special Report." *Current Events*. January 23, 1995.

The Renard. Menasha, Wisconsin: St. Mary High School, 1955.

WBAY's Archives. "A Day with Eddy Jason" television program (1950s). Green Bay, Wisconsin: WBAY-TV production, 1995.

Made in the USA
Charleston, SC
02 January 2014